English in Evidence

Reading and Responding
for GCSE Coursework

John Seely

Heinemann Educational Books

HEINEMANN EDUCATIONAL BOOKS LTD
22 Bedford Square, London WC1B 3HH

LONDON EDINBURGH MELBOURNE AUCKLAND
SINGAPORE KUALA LUMPUR NEW DELHI IBADAN NAIROBI
JOHANNESBURG PORTSMOUTH (NH) KINGSTON

First published in 1987
Reprinted 1987 (twice).

Designed by KAG Design Limited, Basingstoke

Cover illustration of Japanese woodblock print c 1900 reproduced courtesy of
Dermot de Courcy Robinson

ISBN 0 435 10800 X

Printed in Great Britain by
Butler & Tanner Ltd, Frome and London

Contents

Introduction

English in Evidence provides study and practice material for two important elements of the GCSE examination.

GCSE requires the student to be able to read and understand non-literary material presented in a variety of forms. These may include advertisements, journalism, statistics and other tabulated information, graphs and diagrams. Secondly it tests the ability to write in 'closed' situations, 'where the subject matter, form, audience, and purpose are largely "given"'. The examining groups have interpreted these two major requirements in different ways, but they are both present in all options offered, whether partly exam-based or 100 per cent coursework. The Southern Examining Group Syllabus A, for example, states that Paper 2 'will require candidates to produce directed writing in response to material ... which may include information in statistical or graphical form [and which] will present candidates with a situation requiring a variety of tasks'. Such work is different in both intention and detail from what many teachers and classes have been accustomed to. *English in Evidence* provides material to prepare students for this element of GCSE. The book is divided into three parts: *Techniques*, *Sample Units* and *Practice Units*.

Part A: Techniques provides an introduction to the types of material that will be encountered in the rest of the book, and to the kinds of response that are required. There are four main elements: *data*, *visuals*, *words*, and the social and linguistic context in which these occur, the *situation*. The four units in Part A deal with each of these in turn. They analyse and practise the skills required in the rest of the book.

Part B: Sample Units then shows six different ways in which these skills of understanding and expression may be tested. These units are based on the kind of material which examining groups use in formal examinations and which many teachers like to use in coursework. Each unit is preceded by a brief explanatory introduction. The assignments at the end of each are graded. They begin with simple short activities and build up to directed writing tasks requiring a fuller and more independent response on the part of the student.

Part C: Practice Units provides sixteen units which develop and extend the six types illustrated in Part B. On the Contents Page these are categorised so that students can see how they relate to the Sample Units. The Practice Units are graded according to difficulty and provide a full range of activities from simple questions to full and detailed directed writing assignments.

Part A
Techniques

EVENING
ECHO

RIVER RESCUE
HERO SAVED
INSTRUCTOR

PROGRESS
CONTROLLER

...MALS
have rights

5th Forms

	MON	TUES	WED	THURS	FRI
9.55	Maths	French	Class. St.	English	Class. St.
-10.35	French	English	French	Germ.	Germ.
3 .35-11.15	Chem.	Germ.	Maths	R.E.	Chem.
11.15-11.35	BREAK				
4 11.35-12.15	P.E.	Maths	Physics	French	English
5 12.15-12.55	Hist	Maths	Germ.	Chem.	Maths
12.55-2.10	DINNER TIME				
6 2.10-2.50	Physics	Hist.	Bio.	Art	Games
7 2.50-3.30	Physics	Bio.	English	Art	Games
HOMEWORK	Physics French Hist.	Maths English German	English R.E. Bio.	Art Germ. French	Chem. Class.St. Maths

I was, therefore, extremely surprised and upset when I recently opened a copy of our magazine, to find an [ar]ticle by Susie Finchley [whi]ch not only claimed to [be w]holly original but also [gave the] impression that all [the ba]ckground research was [carried] out by

Information and ideas come to us in a variety of different ways. In the past the commonest were hearing and reading. Today we rely increasingly on *visual information*: a mixture of words and images. As its use grows, it is more and more important that we should read it accurately and interpret it correctly. The new GCSE examination recognises this and assesses these skills either in coursework or in formal tests. This book gives practice in reading and responding to different kinds of information package.

Assignment

Study the illustration on the previous pages and then work out the answers to these questions:
1 What kind of information or ideas does each item give us?
2 Some of them are meant to *inform*, some to *persuade*. Which does which?
3 How does each item get across its information or ideas?

Part A shows some of the *techniques* needed to deal with visual information accurately and fully. There are four units.

Data

HAYS SCHOOL T/T 1986-7				5th Forms
	MON	TUES	WED	THURS	FRI
1 9.15-9.55	Maths	French	Class. St.	English	Class. St.
2 9.55-10.35	French	English	french	Germ.	Germ.
3 10.35-11.15	Chem.	Germ.	Maths	R.E.	Chem.
11.15-11.35	BREAK				

How to deal with statistics and information that is set out in tables.

Visuals

How to interpret charts, diagrams and pictures.

Words

Special ways in which words are used to inform and persuade.

Writing in a Situation

How language is used in special situations.

Data

We frequently have to use information that is presented in the form of a table.
Your understanding of the information in this table can be tested in a number of ways.

Age Limits

When you are	You can	Special notes
18+	Drink alcohol in a pub	
16+	Drive a moped	
17+	Drive a car	
21+	Drive a heavy goods vehicle	
18+	Vote	
21+	Stand for Parliament	
16+	Join the army	Male (parents' permission needed if under 18)
17+	Join the army	Female (parents' permission needed if under 18)
18½+	Join the police	Full-time
16+	Join the police	As a police cadet
16+	Get married	16 – 18 parents' consent needed in England and Wales
16+	Buy cigarettes	

Assignment

Simple questions
1 How old do you have to be before you can drive a heavy goods vehicle?
2 At what age can you get married without your parents' permission?
3 At what age can you become an MP?

True/false and multiple choice questions
4 Which of these statements is true and which is false?
  (a) Mary is 17 so she can legally join the army without her parents' consent.
  (b) Now Dave is 18½ he can join the police full-time.
5 Which of the statements below are true?
    A (i) and (ii)   B (i) and (iii)
    C (ii) and (iii)   C (i) and (iv)
  (i)   John can't drive a moped yet because he's only 15.
  (ii) Now I'm 20 I can do anything on that list except stand for Parliament.
  (iii) Anne's parents have agreed, so she can join the army as soon as she's 17.
  (iv) Peter and Yvonne are only 17 so even if their parents agree they'll have to get married in Scotland.

Complex questions

6 Has any of the following people committed an offence? If so, explain who and why.

Martin Davies is 17. He borrowed his father's car and drove into town. He went to a kiosk and bought himself some cigarettes and then took his girlfriend to the pub, where they both had a drink. She had a gin and he had a Coca Cola.

Ray Jones is 20. He's had a driving licence for two years. His father is a lorry driver. Sometimes Ray goes with him on trips and takes turns at driving.

Sheila Peters is 16. Without her parents' consent she and her boyfriend went to Edinburgh and got married. When she got back she bought a moped and used it to go to work.

Sometimes your understanding of a set of data may be tested by asking you to use it in a particular way. For example, you might be asked to study the data and then to use them in a piece of directed writing.

TV Schedules

You are a TV programmer. You are working out the schedules for Spring Monday evenings. Study the information provided and then follow the instructions at the end.

Outline schedule

Time	Type of programme required
6.00 p.m.	News, national and local
7.00 p.m.	Chat show
7.30 p.m.	Feature
8.00 p.m.	Quiz show
8.30 p.m.	Series
9.00 p.m.	News
9.30 p.m.	Soap
10.15 p.m.	Sport or current affairs
11.00 p.m.	Film
12.30 a.m./1.15 a.m.	Close down

Material available to choose from

Features, quiz games and chat shows

It's Your Pet Quiz game in which pet owners are set to identify their own pet in a group of similar animals by answering a series of questions (30 mins)

Say Hello Chat show in which there is a new linkperson each week (45 mins)

Play It Again Chat show in which famous sportspeople relive historic sporting moments (30 mins)

Relatively Speaking Quiz game in which members of the same family work as a team against other families (40 mins)

The Year in Question	Feature about the events of a particular year (30 mins)
Follow That Team	Feature based on idea of following a particular sporting team in the course of a normal week of their lives (30 mins)

Series and soaps

Vet a Surprise!	Series about the life of a country vet (30 mins)
Student Princes	Series about lives of a group of upper class students at university (45 minutes)
All Strung Up	Series about lives of professional tennis players (30 minutes)
The Valley	Soap based on lives of people living in a South Wales valley (45 mins)
Big Apple	Soap based on inhabitants of a New York tenement (45 mins)

Sport and current affairs

World Bowls	Finals of world indoor bowls championships (45 mins)
Snooker/Darts	Snooker doubles championship from Sheffield plus top action from first world ladies' darts championship (45 mins)
Probe	TV investigation programme that gets behind the news headlines and probes a matter of national importance (45 mins)
Inner City	Current affairs programme based on problems of the inner city (45 mins)

Assignment

Work out the best combination of programmes to cover the period from 6 p.m. to 11 p.m. Try to get as much interest and variety into your schedule as possible. Make sure that the programmes chosen are of the right length. Write out the schedule and underneath give a short explanation of why you have chosen the items you have.

Statistics

Quite often you will find that you have to read and understand a set of figures. As with other data, you may be tested by having to answer questions, or you may be asked to do a piece of writing. This exercise contains both questions and directed writing.

Holidays

	1971	1976	1984
Holidays taken by residents of Great Britain (in millions)			
(a) In Great Britain	34	38	34
(b) Abroad	7	7	16
Total	41	45	50

Destination of holidays abroad (percentages)	1971	1976	1984
Belgium/Luxembourg	3	3	1
France	10	12	10
Germany	6	5	5
Greece	3	6	6
Irish Republic	6	4	2
Italy	8	10	6
Holland	3	2	2
Austria	7	3	4
Spain/Majorca, etc.	34	29	36
Switzerland	4	2	2
USA	2	3	3
Other	14	21	23

Assignments

Questions

1 The number of holidays taken in Great Britain in 1984 was about the same as the figure for 1971. What has happened to the figures for holidays abroad in the same period?

2 What is the most popular country for holidays abroad?

3 What is the second most popular country?

4 In 1971 the Irish Republic came fifth in popularity as a holiday area. Where did it come in 1984?

5 How many countries have increased in popularity between 1971 and 1984?

Writing

It is 1984. You have been asked by a travel firm to report on changes in British holiday likes and dislikes over the past eight years. Use the information in the table and write a paragraph explaining how tastes in foreign travel have changed.

Visuals

Graphs and Charts

Sometimes it is difficult to take in the full meaning of a set of figures. When we are studying figures we usually want to be able to compare them in some way. There are three convenient visual ways of presenting figures to help the reader understand them.

Graph

A graph is particularly useful when we want to show how a set of figures changes over a period of time.

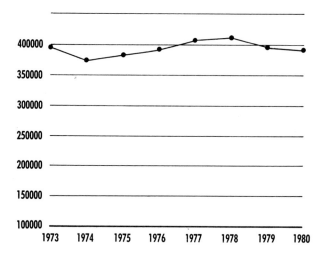

Block chart

A block chart is useful when we want to compare the figures for different things at the same time: for example, the number of people who regularly read different newspapers.

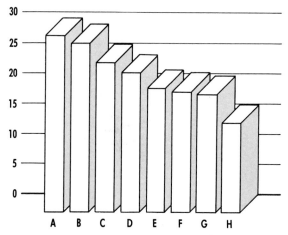

Pie chart

A pie chart is used when we want to see how something is divided up into its different sections.

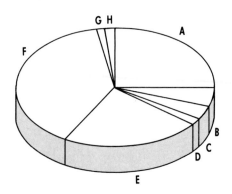

Comparing a block chart and a pie chart

The difference between these two is shown by the example that follows.

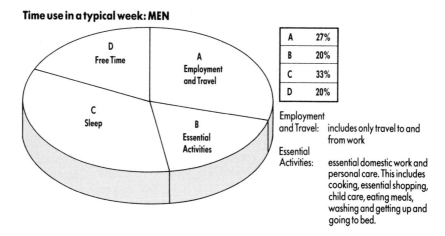

Time use in a typical week: MEN

A	27%
B	20%
C	33%
D	20%

Employment
and Travel: includes only travel to and from work

Essential
Activities: essential domestic work and personal care. This includes cooking, essential shopping, child care, eating meals, washing and getting up and going to bed.

Assignment

Study the pie chart and then answer these questions.
1 Which of the four activities do men devote the most time to?
2 Which of the four has least time devoted to it?
3 Using the percentage figures given, how much time in each period of 24 hours does the average man give to:
(a) employment and travel?
(b) essential activities?
(c) free time?
(d) sleep?

If we want to compare the way in which men and women use their time, it is easier to use a block chart.

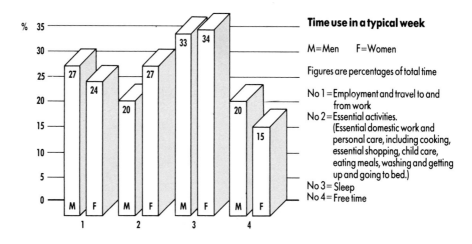

Time use in a typical week

M=Men   F=Women

Figures are percentages of total time

No 1 = Employment and travel to and from work
No 2 = Essential activities.
(Essential domestic work and personal care, including cooking, essential shopping, child care, eating meals, washing and getting up and going to bed.)
No 3 = Sleep
No 4 = Free time

Assignment

Study the block chart and then answer these questions.
1 Which of the four activities do men devote least time to?
2 Which of the four activities do women devote least time to?
3 Approximately how much of each period of 24 hours do women spend on (a) sleep and (b) essential activities?
4 What do you think is the reason for these differences?

Writing about graphs and charts

Sometimes instead of answering questions about a chart, we may be asked to use the information it contains as the basis for a piece of writing.

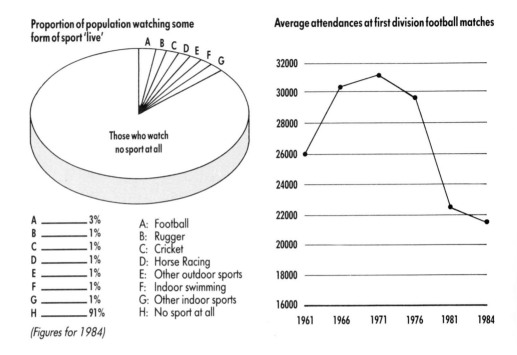

Proportion of population watching some form of sport 'live'

Those who watch no sport at all

A ———— 3%	A: Football	
B ———— 1%	B: Rugger	
C ———— 1%	C: Cricket	
D ———— 1%	D: Horse Racing	
E ———— 1%	E: Other outdoor sports	
F ———— 1%	F: Indoor swimming	
G ———— 1%	G: Other indoor sports	
H ———— 91%	H: No sport at all	

(Figures for 1984)

Average attendances at first division football matches

Assignment

Use the information in the two charts as the basis for a short newspaper article: 'Are We Still a Sporting Nation?'

Diagrams

Books and magazines often use diagrams to make information clearer or give it more impact. Frequently diagrams are used together with words, but sometimes the diagram works on its own.

Where all the heat goes

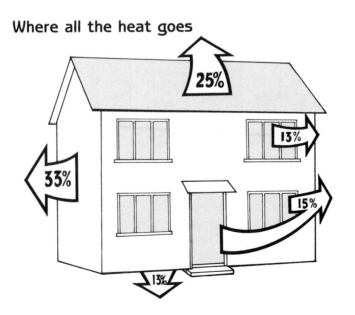

Assignment

1 If you wanted to make the diagram clearer you could add simple labels. Make up labels to go with each of the arrows in the diagram.
2 Use the information in the diagram as the basis for a paragraph explaining how much of the money spent on heating is wasted, and how it could be saved by draughtproofing and insulation. (It is estimated that in an uninsulated house up to 75% of the money spent on heating is wasted in this way.)

Taking good photographs

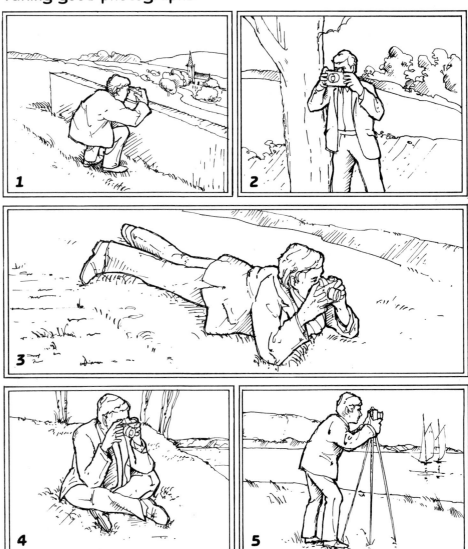

Assignment

These diagrams come from a book about photography. They illustrate how the photographer can make sure that the camera is steady when the photograph is taken, thus avoiding blurred pictures. The pictures are numbered. Write a short explanation for each one.

Photographs

Photographs are frequently used alongside data or text. Sometimes you may need to work purely with one or more photographs and no words or figures at all. This almost always involves interpreting or 'decoding' what is going on in the pictures.

1

2

3

Assignments

Preliminary work
Study the photographs carefully and work out what exactly happened. Write notes on what happened, referring to each of the pictures by its number.

Writing
You are a press reporter who was present at the crash. Write a full report of the incident, with a suitable headline.

Preliminary work

Study the photographs and make notes on each one, reporting on what the area shown is like to live and work in.

Writing

You are a local inhabitant who has lived through all the changes shown in the photographs. Write an article for a local newspaper telling the story of what has happened and how it has affected life in the neighbourhood.

Words

When you are studying a piece of writing, it is useful to begin by deciding on the purpose of the passage. The writing in this book is of two main types.

(a) Writing intended to *inform*:

Canadian-born pop-star Jay-Jay Hammerkopf hit town today. Jay-Jay is here to promote her latest series of personal appearances around Britain followed by a holiday in Paris.

(b) Writing intended to *persuade*:

..... Latest contest, you really must get to see her if you can. She sings these ballads that are so sad.
And she's got this fantastic backing group. I know you'll love her songs and the lyrics are really .....

Sometimes a piece of writing may be intended to inform *and* persuade:

Jay-Jay Hammerkopf's latest offering, *Let's Make It,* has got to be about the draggiest thing this side of Winnipeg – and Winnipeg, in case you don't know it, is a kind of Canadian version of Basingstoke. Winnipeg also happens to be the place where Jay-Jay hails from. Oh well, if you must you must. But just listen to *Let's Make It* and you'll see what I mean. The lyrics are bad and the backing is worse. And that voice . . .!

Seeing the Pattern

When you begin to work on a piece of writing it is useful to do two things:
1   decide the purpose of the writing;
2   get an idea of the *pattern* of the writing.
If you can understand the pattern, you will find it easier to understand the detail later.

Example

The passage that follows was originally printed in a number of paragraphs. Here it is printed as one.

To prove the Goodyear GT is the safest tyre in the wet a very special test was called for. We went to Borrowdale in Cumbria, listed in *The Guinness Book of Records* as the wettest place in Britain. We fitted the Goodyear GT to the cars of over 150 local drivers. At this moment they are putting the GT to the toughest test. The test of everyday motoring in an area known for some of the worst driving conditions. They will then tell us in detail what difference the GT made to their daily driving. Our experience on the test track shows the GT to have unsurpassed grip and control in the wet. A degree of safety, we believe, these drivers will actually feel at the wheel. A relatively short time and many testing miles will prove it.

Goodyear advertisement

Q *What is the purpose?*
A To inform and persuade.

Q *What are the main things it is about?*
A Three things: Borrowdale, their 'experiment', what they think of their tyres.

Q *So what is the pattern?*
A It is in four parts:

1 Introduction
2 What they did
3 Why they did it
4 What they expect to find out

Assignment

Now answer the same questions for this passage.

When I first met Erna she was building a road block. She and her neighbours were struggling to wedge an empty oil drum in place with rocks, planks of wood, broken furniture and bags of rubbish. It was little more than a gesture, perhaps, for access to their street had already been blocked by an overturned metropolitan bus, still smouldering from the fire that had destroyed it. 'When they shift that bus they've still got us to deal with,' she remarked grimly. It was January 15, 1985, the day Prime Minster of Jamaica, Edward Seaga, announced that the prices of petrol, diesel oil and kerosene would increase by 20 per cent. Erna was just one of the thousands of Jamaicans who reached the limits of their endurance and took to the streets in protest. 'I've never been a member of any political party, and probably never will be, but this government is too much. We've had enough,' she explained as we retreated out of the midday sun on to her verandah.

New Internationalist, September 1985

Your understanding of a piece of writing can be tested by a variety of different types of question. The main ones are illustrated in this section. Read the passage and then answer the questions.

My Marathon — by Jimmy Savile

God willing, the 1986 London event will be my 50th marathon. As it happens, my very first officially-timed marathon was the first-ever London event in 1981. So what is it about these races that get tens of thousands of people to run all the 26.2 miles and millions of spectators to stand for up to five hours in all weathers?

It's easy to find the reason for football, tennis or cricket. They are competitive games and the spectators have favourites they hope will win. The London Marathon has 20,000 runners but a million spectators will cheerfully stand and watch a procession of 19,999 losers. The runners' reason is in a word – excitement. The operative word for the spectators must be – spectacle.

For those of us lucky enough to run the distance, the night before a big race, with its world-wide TV audience, is unbearable. Broken sleep, deep nervous breathing, non-stop talking as the day dawns and constant checking everything is all right.

In all my marathons I have never stood on the start when everything has been all right. On the line at one of the Glasgow marathons and standing next to me is Lesley Watson, surely the most attractive world champion lady athlete. Running my eyes over her body, which I am prone to do, I ask why she is not wearing her number. 'Goodness,' she says, 'I've forgotten to put it on.'

A bonus for one who is about to be left on the line is the sight of much fiddling with pins in personal areas. One of my team made five visits to the toilet in the half hour before the start of the race at Whitley Bay, Tyne and Wear, and in the first five miles of any race the world is treated to the sight of several hundred gents lined up using any available wall.

Another reason for so many participants is the super feeling that comes with being fit. There is an enormous gap between being healthy and being fit.

In a recent TV interview, Ron Clarke – the great Australian record-breaker now living in England – mentioned his everlasting memory of the sheer excitement of feeling fit as he was running free. It's an amazing feeling and once you've tasted it nothing else will do. It's even better than romance. Last year I took off for a cruise on the fabulous QE2. After three days of good food, sun and fun but no run, it all became too much. As the passengers sat down for lunch I took off and ran 65 times round the promenade deck, just over 13 miles, and got to the dining room in time for the nosh.

Jimmy Savile, *Weekend*, 22 April

Assignment

Preliminary questions

1 What is the purpose of this piece of writing?
2 What are the main things it is about?
3 What is the pattern?

Questions about factual detail

4 How many marathons had Jimmy Savile run at the time he wrote the article?
5 How many people run in the London Marathon?
6 He describes how marathon runners feel the night before a big race.
 Name two of the effects it has.
7 Who is Lesley Watson?
8 Where is Whitley Bay?
9 Who is Ron Clarke?
10 What does Ron Clarke think is the most important thing about running?

Questions asking you to generalise

You should not quote from the passage in answering these questions.

11 In the first paragraph Jimmy Savile asks himself a question.
Explain it in your own words.
12 How do marathon runners feel on the night before a big race?
13 Why does the writer tell the story about Lesley Watson forgetting her number?
14 How do marathon runners behave just before the start of a marathon?

Questions requiring deduction

15 When Jimmy Savile started on the 1986 London Marathon for how many years had he been running officially timed events?
16 How far is it *once* round the promenade deck of the QE2?

Questions requiring deduction and generalisation

17 How does Jimmy Savile feel about marathon running?
18 What is your evidence for this?
19 What are his reasons for feeling like this?

Summarising

20 Using the information contained in the article write a paragraph of 120-150 words about the pleasures and problems of marathon running.

Directed Writing

Frequently your skill in understanding a text will be one of a number of skills tested by a directed writing assignment. The exercise that follows contains examples of directed writing.

Summer Challenge!

Are you resourceful, hardworking and patient, with a strong sense of humour? Are you between the ages of 15 and 20? Have you got four weeks to spare this summer during the school holidays? Are you prepared to take on a real challenge and do something useful at the same time?
Do you like holidays at the seaside or in the Lake District?

If the answer to all these questions is 'Yes', then you are just the person we are looking for to help us. We need your skills and interests to help us run holidays for handicapped youngsters between the ages of 8 and 12 on the South Coast and near Lake Windermere. We can't offer anything glamorous, just a lot of hard work, fresh air and the satisfaction that you are helping to make someone's life happier and more worthwhile. We pay expenses plus a small weekly allowance. Board and lodging are free. If you are interested, write us a letter, telling us about yourself and why you think you are the kind of person we're looking for.
Helping Hand Holidays
Fellows Farm
Bartesford
Wilts WR4 6TY

Assignment

1 Write a letter in reply to the advertisement.
2 The following are among the letters received in reply. You have been given the task of reading them and deciding how suitable each person is. Read them and write notes explaining your views on each writer and how suitable he or she is for the work offered.

I am in the fifth form at Borthwick School, Upper Barton, Leicestershire and am studying 6 subjects for the exams. I'm not particularly brainy but I am very keen on outdoor activities. As well as all the sports we do at school I take part in sailing and mountaineering whenever I can and have been on several Youth Hostelling holidays with the school. At our school we have quite a lot of handicapped children who have lessons with the rest of the school and are cared for by a specialist Support Unit. A number of us help the Support Unit during dinner break and after school pushing wheelchairs, helping them with sports and so on – so I think I've got a bit of experience which might come in useful.

I'd like to go on one of the holidays you are offering. I'd like to go to the Lake District, because I've never had the chance to go there and I think I'd enjoy it. I don't mind about the money. I'm quite good with people – I've got a lot of friends and we're always having a good laugh. I'm interested in biking and rock music. I hope you'll take me on.

I am in my last year at Brantick High School, an 11–16 comprehensive. I am taking 7 subjects at GCSE and hope next year to go on to the sixth form college to study Maths, Physics and Music. I am a school prefect and captain of my House Hockey and Netball teams. I like athletics and swimming. I don't get much spare time, but when I do, my interests are computers and reading, as well as playing the viola. I think I could help quite well on one of your holidays, because although I am a fairly quiet person, I am very patient and I am prepared to work hard. My parents told me I ought to write to you and I think the experience would be very good for me.

Writing in a Situation

Sometimes, when working on units like those in this book, you will be asked to write 'inside' a situation:

> You are the manager of the supermarket. Write a report about the shoplifting incident.

or

> You are the organiser of this year's festival. Write a letter to a well-known TV personality asking him or her to open the festival.

Assignments like these ask for a special kind of writing. What you write and how you write it are affected by two main things:

1 who is writing and to whom;
2 what you are writing about.

Writer and Audience

The writer and the audience affect both the words that are used and the way they are used.

...for your second interview. You should attend at this office at...

Assignment

1 Write the full text of each of the three letters in the illustration.
2 For each of the examples that follows, explain who the writer is, who the audience is to be and your reasons for thinking this.

Which is why, by the end of the fourteenth century, the population of England had fallen by about 50 per cent.

Quite accurate but rather an abrupt ending — what about the effects of this on the reign of Richard II?

14/20

I shall be very glad to allow you and two friends from school to visit the House and to be shown round. If you would like to come, I will let me know when you would like to come, I will make the necessary arrangements.

The area behind the science block is out of bounds until further notice. Anyone found in this area without permission will be punished. No excuses will be accepted.

I regret to inform you that your account has been overdrawn for two weeks, by the sum of £45.74. Should you wish proper overdraft facilities, I shall, of course, be very pleased to discuss the matter with you. In the meantime ...

3 Write three short accounts of the following incident:
   (a) by the policewoman, reporting it at the police station;
   (b) by one of the two girls, in a note to her mother explaining why she will be late home;
   (c) by a person in the street who saw what happened and is writing about it to the local paper.

What You Are Writing About

Every subject has its own special language. Often we use the language of a particular subject without being aware that it is special.

Assignments

1 Write a short description of a disco, that can be understood by someone (e.g. from another country) who has never been to a disco.
2 Think of the subjects that you are studying for the exams. Each has its own special vocabulary. Choose two subjects and make lists of words and phrases that are special to that subject.

Sometimes it is necessary to pick up the language of a subject in order to be able to write or talk about it.

Assignment

You have a friend who works in a large bank. One day she shows you round the office in which she works. Describe what happens. Use the information in this illustration to help you.

Part B
Sample Units

Visuals — Our Changing Town
Words and Pictures — The Country Code
Journalism — Terrorism
Advertising — Data Link
Simulation — Road Traffic Accident
Issues — What Did You Learn In School Today?

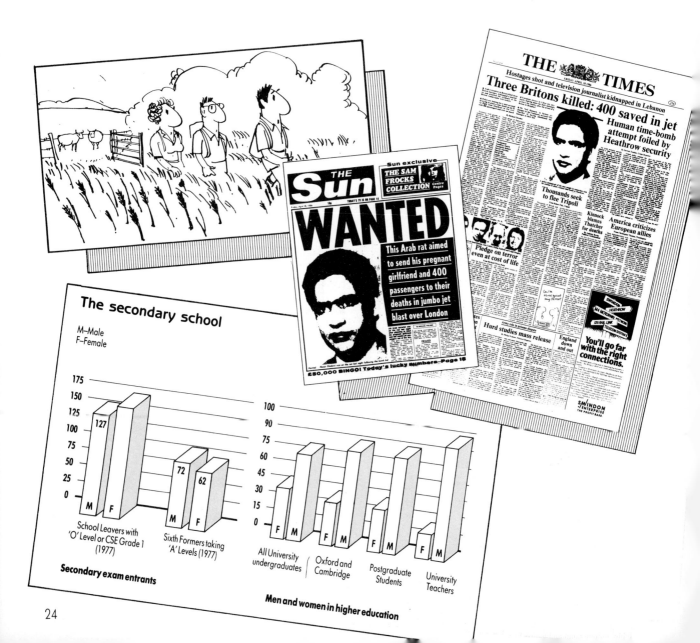

25

Visuals

Sometimes all the information in a package is contained in photographs, drawings or diagrams. You are then asked to 'read' the information and write about it in different ways.

Our Changing Town

Assignments

Preparatory work
Questions about photograph A

1 What methods of transport are shown in use?
2 What time of day do you think it is?
3 What are the main buildings you can see, and what is their purpose?
4 What would you say were the main activities in this part of the city?

Questions about photograph B

5 What methods of transport are shown in use in this photograph?
6 What time of day is it?
7 What are the main buildings and what do you think they are used for?
8 What are the main activities in this part of the city?

Questions about both photographs

9 What changes do you observe in the following?
   (a) types of building
   (b) road layout
   (c) the purpose the area is used for
10 What is the most important change that has taken place?

Writing

1 Write factual descriptions of the two photographs and comment on the ways in which the area has changed.
2 *Either:*
   (a) A city guide is being produced. It will contain the two photographs and a short but enthusiastic article about the changes that have taken place. Write the article.
   Or:
   (b) Imagine that you are a person who used to live in this city at the time of photograph A. You moved away and did not revisit the area. Then you came back to it at the time of photograph B. Write an account of your thoughts and feelings as you look at the new scene.

A

B

Words and Pictures

Often pictures are combined with words. The pictures are not just a decoration; they provide essential information. This unit is based on a publication which uses pictures in this way. As you can see, something has gone wrong.

The Country Code

More people than ever before enjoy exploring the countryside. This Code has been written to help you get all the pleasure you can from the countryside while contributing to its care.

A

1 Fire

In summertime when it is most pleasant to be outdoors there is always a risk of fire. Hay, heathland and bracken can catch light so easily and once ablaze are very hard to put out. A little care is all that's needed. Care with lighted cigarettes, pipes or matches. Care in preparing that campsite or barbecue. Don't run the risk of starting something that you can't stop, and remember—fire spreads so quickly.

B

2 Gates

Gates are there to prevent farm animals from straying either out of or into an enclosure. It is often just as important to keep them out of one field as it is to keep them in another. So, to be safe, always close and fasten a gate behind you, even if it was open when you found it—it may have been left open by accident.

C

3 Dogs

Even if he's just playing, a dog which chases cows or sheep can do a great deal of harm and if there are young animals, calves or lambs, about, they can easily be killed. The fact that the dog didn't mean any harm is no excuse. Both you and your dog will enjoy your walk more if he's under control. If there is livestock about there's only one sure place for him. On the lead.

D

4 Paths

There are more than 100,000 miles of public paths providing rights of way throughout Britain. They will be clearly marked on your Ordnance Survey map and many of them are waymarked and signposted. Make sure that you keep to the path and you can be sure you are not trespassing. You will be treading in the footsteps of generations of countrymen.

E

5 Livestock, crops, machinery

Crops and machinery are best left alone. Farm animals are best viewed from a distance so as not to disturb them. Farming today is a major industry and a very complex one. Chance factors such as weather play a big part in the success or failure of a season's crops. It is better to take no chances and to avoid interfering with farm work.

F

6 Litter

Everyone likes a picnic. It's one of the best things about a day out in the country. Children, especially, revel in eating outdoors. Make sure you don't spoil it for yourself and others by leaving unsightly litter. Modern packaging materials like plastics don't rot or decay. They stay around and look unpleasant and can often harm wildlife and farm animals. It's easy to take an empty bag with you and take your litter home.

G

7 Roads

Roads in the country serve many users. Round a tree-lined corner you could find a slow-moving tractor, a flock of sheep, children on their bicycles or a party of ramblers. If you are in a car, take extra care, be patient and drive slowly. If you wish to park, make sure that you do not block a farm gateway. Horse riders and cyclists need special consideration, a slow speed and a wide berth.

H

PICNIC AREA

8 Noise

Most animals are very timid. Sudden or loud noises can disturb them unnecessarily. Wild animals are so shy that at the slightest noise they will disappear altogether. If you want to get the best out of the country go quietly. Stop frequently and listen to the life around you. To see the countryside at its best you have to try to be part of it, to disturb it as little as possible and take nothing from it but happy memories.

Assignments

1. The pictures on pages 28-30 are supposed to match the text, but they have been jumbled up. Which picture goes with which rule?
2. Each picture should have a short caption, stating the rule clearly in a few words. Make up a caption for each picture.
3. The cartoons below show some of the rules being broken.
    Explain clearly what is wrong in each picture and why.
4. The cartoons do not show all of the rules being broken. Take two of the rules not illustrated and make up one or two cartoons showing these being broken. Aim to make your cartoons amusing but also instructive. If you are not very good at drawing, write a detailed description of what is in your cartoon(s), so that an artist could follow it.
5. Choose up to three of the rules listed and make up a poster to illustrate them. Your poster should be aimed at young children and should bring home to them clearly and simply the point of these rules.
6. You have been asked to help with a country camping holiday for a group of 10-year-olds. You have to explain to them that they should respect the countryside and the people who work there. Make up a short talk explaining this, using the material on pages 28-30.

Journalism

This unit gives practice in comparing and writing about newspaper stories. It shows you how to see differences in:

1 style;
2 content;
3 presentation.

Terrorism

Newspapers often run the beginning of a story on the front page and then continue it on a later page. They usually place the part of the story they think most important on the front page. The two extracts that follow are from the front page stories in *The Times* and the *Sun*. The paragraphs are numbered for use in the exercises that follow.

Human time-bomb attempt foiled by Heathrow security

1 An Arab terrorist secretly planted a time bomb in the luggage of his pregnant girlfriend, planning to use her as a human time-bomb to kill more than 400 passengers on an El Al flight from London to Tel Aviv yesterday.

2 The 10lb bomb, timed to explode after the Boeing 747 took off, was hidden in a false bottom in the woman's holdall. It was discovered when she arrived at an El Al security check in Terminal One at Heathrow airport yesterday morning.

3 The woman, who is southern Irish and in her late twenties, worked as a hotel cleaner in London, where she met the Arab a year ago.

4 She was on her way to Israel, where the Arab said he would marry her. He had told her he could not travel on El Al as he was an Arab, but would follow on a later plane.

5 The alarm was raised when El Al staff searching the bag became suspicious but the woman's boyfriend, named by Scotland Yard as Nezar Hindawi, had vanished.

6 Armed police combed the airport as explosives experts worked in Terminal One to disarm the bomb but the Arab had vanished.

7 Police are unsure whether he is still in Britain or swiftly escaped on a flight to Europe and all airlines at Heathrow were asked to check passenger lists.

8 The Yard's anti-terrorist branch issued a description of the Arab yesterday as they continued to question the woman.

9 Commander George Churchill-Coleman, head of the anti-terrorist branch, said there was a very real possibility that the girl had been duped by her boyfriend and there was no question of charging her at the moment.

10 Mr Churchill-Coleman said the bomb was an 'improvised explosive device ... it was viable and would have exploded once the aircraft was airborne. It is highly likely that it would have resulted in the loss of the aircraft and the 400 passengers and crew.'

11 The police have refused to give any details of the man apart from saying that he visited London from time to time but they issued a photograph.

12 He is described as 5ft 10in tall with black curly hair, greying at the sides.

The Times, 18 April 1986

WANTED

This Arab rat aimed to send his pregnant girlfriend and 400 passengers to their deaths in jumbo jet blast over London

1 **An Arab terrorist was on the run last night after planning to blast his pregnant girlfriend and 400 Jumbo jet passengers out of the sky.**

2 The girl – unaware of the danger – was held yesterday at London's Heathrow Airport.

3 Her lover kissed her goodbye – then fled seconds before she was due to board an El Al plane bound for Israel with a 10lb bomb hidden in her holdall.

4 Last night the sobbing girl, an Irish hotel worker, was being interrogated by Scotland Yard's detectives – shocked that the man had been prepared to send her and their baby to certain death.

PRIMED

5 And a massive international hunt was launched for the Arab rat, 35-year-old Jordanian journalist Nezar Hindawi.

6 Police believe he has gone to ground in either London or Paris.

7 The bomb was almost certainly meant for an Arab revenge attack following the blitzing of Libya.

8 It was primed to explode soon after take-off using an air-pressure device.

9 Detectives said it would have destroyed the Jumbo and slaughtered all 400 passengers and crew.

10 The blast would almost certainly have happened as the plane was climbing over London.

11 And hundreds could have been killed if the jet had plummeted into busy streets.

Sun, 18 April 1986

Assignments

Preparatory work

1 Make notes on the visual appearance of the two news stories.
Compare the following:
   (a) how much of the front page each takes up;
   (b) the use made of pictures;
   (c) the use made of headlines and how big they are.

2 Make notes on the content of each story. For each one, write the number of each paragraph and a word or phrase summing up what it contains. (For example, for *The Times* one you might begin: '(1) Summary of plan. (2) The bomb.')

3 Compare the order in which the two versions tell the story. Make notes on any important differences.

4 Copy and complete the following chart:

Words/phrases used to describe:	The Times	Sun
(a) the woman		
(b) the man		
(c) the bomb		
(d) the plane		
Information and ideas contained in one and not the other		

These notes and the chart can now be used to help you with the written assignments.

Writing

1 Write a detailed comparison of the way in which the two newspapers treat the story. You should compare content, style and visual appearance.

2 The main features of how the story developed in the next two days were as follows.
  (a) Nezar Hindawi was arrested in London.
  (b) He was taken to the maximum security police station at Paddington Green.
  (c) He was detained and questioned.
  (d) The girl was held for 48 hours after being arrested.
  (e) During this time she was questioned, but she was not charged.
  (f) Then she was released and the police said that they had no intention of charging her.

Write two short news items containing some or all of this information, one in the style of *The Times* and one in the style of the *Sun*.

Advertising

Printed advertisements are a mixture of visuals and words, combining information and persuasion. They may try to influence the reader in ways that are far from obvious, or they may be more straightforward. When studying and writing about advertisements we need to think about the following.

1 **Overall appearance.** An advertisement depends a lot on its first impact on the reader. This is achieved visually.

2 **Key words and images.**

3 **Information:** the facts about the product.

4 **Open persuasion:** the reasons the advertisement gives explaining why we should buy the product.

5 **Hidden persuasion:** the less obvious ways in which the advertisement tries to persuade us. For example, an advertisement may show a fast car being driven by a handsome young man with an attractive girl. This may lead us to believe, without being aware of it, that if we buy that car we will be sexually successful.

Assignments

Preparatory work

Make notes in answer to these questions:

1 At whom is the advertisement aimed? (There are two possible answers to this: the people it *says* it is aiming at, and the people you think will be attracted by it.)
2 Explain in detail what Datalink offers its customers.
3 It gives a list of reasons why it is a better organisation than others. Sum up the main points it makes.
4 It uses parts of letters from satisfied customers. What are the main points that these make?
5 It offers a *free computer test*. Explain the main point of this.
6 What are the key images and key words of the advertisement?
7 What is your opinion of the design of the advertisement: its use of visuals, layout, kinds of print, etc.?
8 What is your opinion of the questionnaire it contains? Do you think it would give a good enough picture of an applicant's personality? Are there important questions it fails to ask?
9 Does it seek to use any kind of hidden persuasion? In particular does it appeal to secret wishes or fears that people may have which they may be unwilling to admit to or may even be unaware of?

Activities

1 Comment on the style, content and approach of the advertisement. You should describe what the advertisement is selling and to whom; the approach it uses; its main selling line(s); and comment on how effective it is and why.

2 Datalink uses advertisements in local newspapers. Clearly they often aren't as large or expensive as this one in a national magazine. Design a shorter version of the advertisement for a local newspaper, so that it will fit into a space not larger than 5cm by 10cm.

3 The short questionnaire is intended to give a general idea of an applicant's personality. For more accurate use of a computer for matching people, it would be necessary to use a more detailed questionnaire. Make up a list of questions designed to match people according to their personalities, likes and dislikes.

4 You have just taken over responsibility for advertising Datalink.
You are not satisfied with its magazine advertisements.
Either:
(a) write a detailed explanation for the advertising agency explaining what is wrong with the present advertisement and what you want done about it;
or:
(b) design a new advertisement.

Simulation

In a simulation you are asked to imagine that you are taking part in a real life situation. You take on the role of someone in that situation and you read and write as if you were that person. In this simulation you are a police officer investigating and reporting on a road accident.

Road Traffic Accident

Date of incident: 15 March 1986
Report timed at 10.22 a.m.
Report by WPC Atkinson

Statement by Mrs O'Rourke

'I was just walking along the road towards Witney. It was a bit wet – with drizzle, you know — and I couldn't see far ahead at all. Then suddenly out of nowhere there's this red car coming towards me, going like a bat out of hell. He must have been doing at least sixty. Well of course he sees the tractor standing there at the side of the road, but it's too late to stop or anything. His brakes go on with a great noise and at the same time he swerves out round the tractor, but there's this other car, the blue one, you see, in the middle of the road – turning right, I suppose. Anyway he swerves the other way, but it's too late. He had no chance, no chance at all ...'

Statement by Mr J. Norton

'I was just moving my tractor from Down End Field back to the far – that's a bit further along the road towards Oxford. Suddenly it just stopped. Wouldn't budge. I think the engine's seized up. I tried to get it going again but it was no good. So I walked on along the road to the farm – that's Pargeter's Farm, Lower Sandon – to ring the garage for help. There's was nothing else I could do about the tractor. I know it's a dangerous place but what could I do? Tractors don't have hazard lights or anything.'

Vehicles Involved in Accident

Vehicle A
Blue Austin Metro, registration A702TCJ. One occupant, Mrs B. Carter. Injuries suffered: bruise to right forearm, slight shock.

Vehicle B
Red Ford Escort XJI, registration D193AEV. One occupant. Injuries suffered: multiple fractures, probable concussion, unconscious. Not wearing seatbelt.

Vehicle C
John Deere tractor, no number plate, apparently parked at side of road.

Road Layout

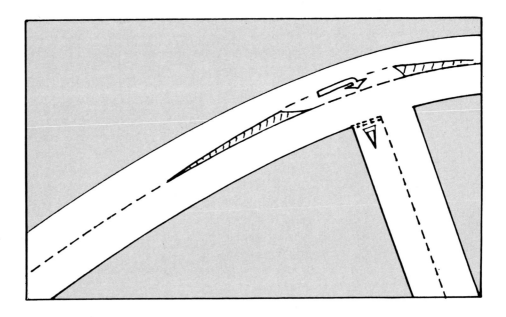

Additional information:	Speed limit of 40 m.p.h.

Additional information: Speed limit of 40 m.p.h.
Weather — overcast with drizzle
Visibility — 100 yards
Road surface — wet and slightly greasy

✱ marks position Mrs O'Rourke says she was in at the time of the accident.

Assignments

Preparatory work

1 Study all the material and make brief notes on the most important points that strike you.

2 Concentrate on Car A and its driver Mrs Carter. Work out:
(a) how her car came to be in the position shown on the plan;
(b) what she would have seen (and heard) of the accident;
(c) whether there was anything she could have done to avoid the accident.
Write brief note-form answers to the above questions.

3 Now focus on Car B and its driver. Make notes on these questions:
(a) How should the weather conditions have caused him to drive?
(b) What other factors were there affecting speed and care at this point on the road?
(c) Was he committing any offences in the way he was driving his car?
(d) Given the conditions and the speed he was travelling at, was there anything he could have done once he saw the tractor?
(e) What is your opinion about the way in which he was driving and his responsibility for the accident?

4 Finally look at the position of the tractor and the statement of Mr Norton. Make notes about these points:
(a) Are there are any further questions you would like to ask him?
(b) Could he have done anything else about the position of his tractor and the danger it caused to other traffic?

Writing

1 The other witness to the accident was Mrs B. Carter, driver of the blue car. She also makes a statement. Work out what her version of the accident will be and write her statement. Remember that you are writing what Mrs Carter says. The picture should give you some idea of what she is like as a person, and therefore how she might speak.

2 WPC Atkinson has to write a full report about the accident. She includes the sketch plans on pages 40 and 41. Use the notes you have made to write her report. This is a formal piece of writing. It will be read by a senior officer. It should be concise, accurate, impersonal. Include all the information that you think is relevant. Add any opinions you may have about how each of the three drivers has behaved.

Issues

Sometimes words, data and visuals are used to put across an argument, or present an important issue. In this unit the subject matter is sexism.

What Did You Learn in School Today? _____

From primary days on, school plays an increasingly important part in sex-role stereotyping. Even if, at the end of your school career, you think you can say with complete certainty that 'I never learned a thing at school' or 'I've forgotten everything I was ever taught' you will be wrong. This might be true of subjects, but not of those things you are taught without being fully aware that you are learning them; what you are taught in school, and what you cannot easily unlearn, is that males and females are different and unequal.

You may object to this and say, but surely everyone — boy or girl — is treated the same at school? On the surface there doesn't seem to be any immediately obvious difference. But if you look more closely at what you are taught and who teaches you, at what is expected of you, or at what you are discouraged from doing, you will begin to see that there are differences.

And once you see them, you are in a better position to do something about them. In your school, in the practical subjects, are girls kept mainly to needlework and home economics, and boys to woodwork, metalwork and technical drawing? If this is so, have you ever asked why?

In some schools boys are encouraged to do *some* needlework and girls to do *a little* metalwork, but is it to the same extent?

Have you ever wanted to take a subject at school but weren't allowed to because of your sex? Was there anything you could do about it?

The organisation of your school

Even if you go to a mixed school, the girls are still separated from the boys by various devices. In some schools you will find these situations:

The register   Boys' and girls' names in separate lists with the boys first.

Lining up   Schoolchildren are so used to being told to line up according to sex, in the playground and outside classrooms, that even when they are given no specific instructions they still do it.

Competition   Group work; for the teacher the simple way out is to say 'boys against girls'. Competition is encouraged along sex lines partly because boys often hate having girls on their side and vice versa.

Uniform   The girls' uniform is always a skirt, never trousers. Even female teachers are discouraged from wearing trousers by many education authorities. Imagine how much your freedom of movement is restricted by having to wear a skirt.

School rules   Among them are restrictions as to length of hair — especially directed against the boys. The less they look like girls the better, presumably.

Separate playgrounds   So that the delicate girls can be protected from rough boys. Or, in mixed playgrounds, boys take over while girls stand in small groups around the edge.

Separate gymnasia   One for each sex is a common feature of large schools. Girls dance and do 'keep fit' exercises in theirs, while the boys play volleyball or something equally strenuous in theirs. Often there are no mixed teams, and separate tuition and instructors.

Assemblies   Girls sit while boys stand — presumably training them for their future role as protectors of the weaker sex. Or if the whole assembly is allowed to sit, then it's the males along one half of the hall, the females along the other.

Outings   How many of them are 'girls only' or 'boys only', with the girls being taken round the local nursery, while the boys visit the steelworks?

People who work in school

Look around your school. Chances are that the teachers and staff are separated along sex lines in the jobs done.

Does the following pattern hold good in your school?

Head teacher: male

Deputy: male or female

Cleaning staff: female

Kitchen staff: female

'Dinner ladies': female

Schoolkeeper: male

Heads of houses or years: male

Deputy heads of houses or years: female or male

School nurses: female

Clerical staff, typists: female

Heads of the maths, geography, science, woodwork/metalwork departments: male

Heads of the needlework and home economics departments: female

The primary school

The following chart is an analysis of sex roles in reading schemes widely used in schools for teaching children how to read.

THE CHILDREN'S ROLES

	Toys and Activities pets		Taking the lead in joint activities	Learning a new skill	The adult roles shown
Girls only	1. Doll 2. Skipping rope 3. Doll's pram	1. Preparing the tea 2. Playing with dolls 3. Taking care of younger siblings	1. Hopping 2. Shopping with parents 3. Skipping	1. Taking care of younger siblings	1. Mother 2. Aunt 3. Grandmother
Boys only	1. Car 2. Train 3. Aeroplane 4. Boat 5. Football	1. Playing with cars 2. Playing with trains 3. Playing football 4. Lifting or pulling heavy objects 5. Playing cricket 6. Watching adult males in occupational roles 7. Heavy gardening	1. Going exploring alone 2. Climbing trees 3. Building things 4. Taking care of pets 5. Sailing boats 6. Flying kites 7. Washing and polishing Dad's car	1. Taking care of pets 2. Making/ building 3. Saving/ rescuing people or pets 4. Playing sports	1. Father 2. Uncle 3. Grandfather 4. Postman 5. Farmer 6. Fisherman 7. Shop or business owner 8. Policeman 9. Builder 10. Bus driver 11. Bus conductor 12. Train driver 13. Railway porter

→

THE CHILDREN'S ROLES

	Toys and Activities pets	Taking the lead in joint activities	Learning a new skill	The adult roles shown
Both Sexes	1. Book 2. Ball 3. Paints 4. Buckets and spade 5. Dog 6. Cat 7. Shop	1. Playing with pets 2. Writing 3. Reading 4. Going to the seaside 5. Going on a family outing		1. Teacher 2. Shop assistant

Glenys Lobban, *Forum for the Discussion of New Trends in Education*

The secondary school

M–Male
F–Female

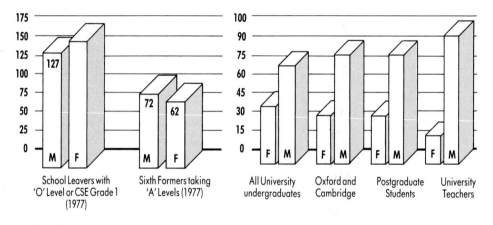

Secondary exam entrants

Men and women in higher education

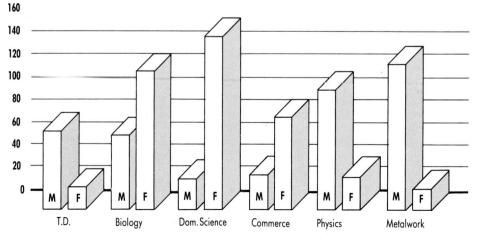

CSE entries 1977

Assignments

Preparatory work

1 Read the 'Recipe'. Which of the points it is making are still true? Are any of them false? Make two lists, headed 'True' and 'False', and give your reasons for placing items in either list.

2 Read the section that begins 'From primary days on ...' and ends '... anything you could do about it?' Then answer these questions:
   (a) The writer makes a distinction between the 'subjects' taught at school and what you really learn. Can you explain this in your own words?
   (b) What is the point of the questions about practical subjects?

3 Read the section entitled 'The organisation of your school'. Now answer these questions:
   (a) How many of these things happen in your school?
   (b) In your school are there any other ways in which boys and girls are separated?

4 Is the pattern in 'People who work in school' true at your school?

5 Read the section entitled 'The primary school'. Make a list of the most important differences between the lists for boys, girls, and both sexes.

6 What do you think should be done to avoid this kind of sex-typing in books for young children?

7 Study the statistics about education. Explain in a few sentences what each of the charts shows.

Writing

1 Make up a new 'Recipe' designed to create not a 'real' man or woman but a 'real person'.

2 Write a set of guidelines entitled 'Equal Opportunities in the Secondary School'. Basing your ideas on the material in the unit, list the main rules which schools should follow in order to avoid the kind of discrimination described in this unit.

3 The book on which this unit is based was first published in 1976 and revised in 1980. Since then things have changed — but by how much? If you were preparing a revised edition, in what ways would you want to change the comments that it makes — apart, of course, from bringing the statistics up to date? Make a list of the items you would wish to change and brief explanations of how you would change them.

4 Write a short story for young children avoiding the problems of sex-typing illustrated in this unit.

Part C
Practice Units

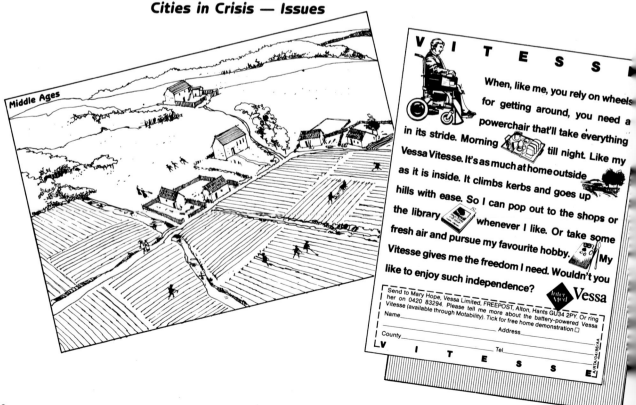

Middle Ages

The scourges of war, repression and inter-communal violence threaten poor people in many of the countries in which Oxfam works. Here we focus on projects working in the shadow of violent conflict.

In 1984–85 Oxfam committed over £300,000 to projects in SOUTH AFRICA. Our policy in South Africa is based on our perception that apartheid is the major obstacle to development for the poor. Here are some of the areas in which we work:

Advice offices — located in black townships or down-city areas, these help people with pension, disability or workers' compensation and with unemployment claims and the problems created by the myriad of apartheid passbook regulations which control black peoples' lives.

Domestic workers — there are an estimated 1 million domestics or "maids" in South Africa and they represent one of the most disadvantaged groups of workers. Oxfam supports the South Africa Domestic Workers Association. Run by former domestic workers, SADWA aims to protect domestics against exploitation and secure fair and reasonable conditions of employment.

Our Changing Village

Studying the pictures

Copy and complete the table, filling in the spaces with a short description of what you can see and the changes that have taken place. Here are the headings you will need for the left-hand column: **Farming** — 1. Fields, 2. Methods; **Countryside around village** (trees, open spaces etc); **Communications** — 1. Roads and paths, 2. River and bridge, 3. Forms of transport; **Buildings** — 1. Ordinary houses, 2. The manor house, 3. The church; **People** — 1. Numbers, 2. Kind of life.

	Middle Ages	18th Century	Modern
FARMING			
1. Fields			
2. Methods			

Writing

Now use your information to write an account of 'Our changing village.'

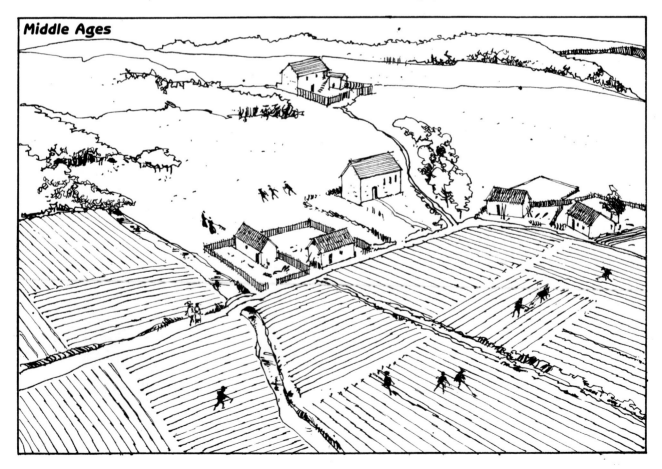

Middle Ages

18th Century

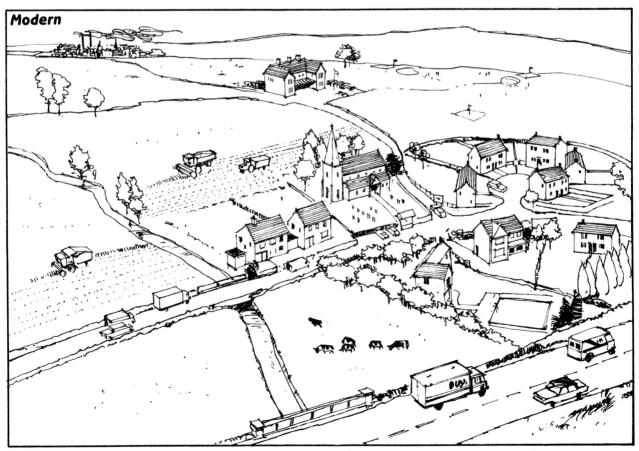

Modern

Caring for the Aged

A

What is Tunstall Lifeline?

Tunstall Lifeline* is a simple to use emergency call unit with modern push button telephone facilities. It plugs into a standard new telephone socket and is mains powered. In the event of a power cut, however, a rechargeable standby battery takes over, supplying power for up to four hours depending on use.

Major Features of Lifeline

● Incorporated into the Lifeline* unit is a large red alarm button which, when pressed, immediately alerts the staff in the 24 hour emergency Control Centre to any potential crisis.

● Lifeline Pendant. The Pendant is an extremely light radio alarm transmitter which can be worn around the neck and is easily concealed under a shirt, blouse or sweater. If for some reason the red alarm button cannot be reached, the button on the Pendant when pressed will do the same job as the alarm button and will activate the emergency system. The Pendant will activate the emergency system from anywhere around the home.

● Two way communication. The most vital part of the Lifeline emergency system. The Lifeline unit has a very powerful in-built loudspeaker that can be heard around the house and an ultra sensitive microphone that is capable of picking up sounds from other rooms. The unit, therefore, allows for two-way speech communication without the use of a handset, although if the caller cannot be heard or is unable to speak the Control Centre operator will call for assistance from a series of predetermined contact numbers.

The Control Centres

The two current Tunstall Lifeline Control Centres are based at Whitley Bridge, Yorkshire and Leatherhead, Surrey. They are staffed 24 hours a day by people experienced in and sympathetic to the problems of the elderly. Every time an emergency call is made, even if the person calling cannot be heard, a computer display indicates exactly who they are, where they live and other essential details.

All Control Centre records and response instructions are treated in the strictest confidence and are only ever used to give immediate help when an emergency call is received.

HELP ON HAND 24 HOURS A DAY

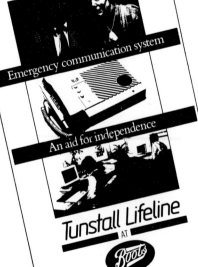

"Even if Mum can't reach the 'phone, she's got immediate help on hand 24 hours a day."

Emergency communication system

An aid for independence

Tunstall Lifeline AT Boots

B

Stairs no longer a problem for Mum or Dad

Easiest and least expensive way to beat stairs. Mum or dad just sits or stands and glides up and down in complete safety. Saves cost of moving home or making alterations. And Stannah offers easy terms or rentals and advises you about grants.

Thousands benefiting. See a Stannah stairlift working. Mum and dad can try it out themselves and meet satisfied users. Push button control. Straight or curved staircases. Installed in hours. No mess. Folds back. Nationwide service. Meets British Standards of Safety.

Fill in coupon below for FREE colour brochure. Post now. No obligation.

Easy terms. FREE Demonstrations.

stannah *powered stairlifts*

Please send FREE colour brochure about Stannah push button stairlifts, including easy terms details.

Name_____

Address_____

_____

Phone_____

Now please post – no stamp needed – to: Stannah Stairlifts National HQ, Dept 5019 FREEPOST, Andover, SP10 3BR. Tel: (0264) 64311 (24hrs).

C

glide upstairs with Stannah

Just sit or stand and glide safely up and down. Saves moving home. See a Stannah stairlift working. Try it yourself. Push button control. Straight or curved stairs. Installed in hours. No mess. Folds back. Stannah advises about grants, terms or rentals.

Send coupon for FREE brochure and demonstration.

Easy Terms. FREE demonstrations.

stannah powered stairlifts

Please send free brochure and arrange free demonstration.

Name _____
Address _____
_____

Phone _____
Please post – no stamp needed – to
Stannah Stairlifts National HQ, Dept 5022
FREEPOST, Andover SP10 3BR.
Tel 0264 64311 (24 hrs).

D

V I T E S S E

When, like me, you rely on wheels for getting around, you need a powerchair that'll take everything in its stride. Morning till night. Like my Vessa Vitesse. It's as much at home outside as it is inside. It climbs kerbs and goes up hills with ease. So I can pop out to the shops or the library whenever I like. Or take some fresh air and pursue my favourite hobby. My Vitesse gives me the freedom I need. Wouldn't you like to enjoy such independence?

InterMed **Vessa**

Send to Mary Hope, Vessa Limited, FREEPOST, Alton, Hants GU34 2PY. Or ring her on 0420 83294. Please tell me more about the battery-powered Vessa Vitesse (available through Motability). Tick for free home demonstration ☐

Name_____ Address_____

County_____ Tel_____

V I T E S S E

E

"You'll L♥ve your Runaround"

"Comfortable, easy to control and reliable". That's the verdict of hundreds of satisfied Runaround owners who had difficulty getting about.
★ Easily re-chargeable battery power with feed back control to maintain safe speeds
★ Cushioned swivel seat with swing back arms
★ Travels most terrain even small kerbs
★ Excellent manoeuvrability indoors or out

Runaround

☐ Please send me a free brochure
☐ I would also like a free home demonstration

Everest & Jennings Ltd, Princewood Rd, Corby, Northants NN17 2DX Tel: Corby (0536) 67661

NAME_____
ADDRESS_____
_____

TEL. NO._____

Everest & Jennings
The Caring Company RT 16

Assignments

Advertisement A

1 Explain briefly the purpose of each of the following and how it works:
(a) the red alarm button;
(b) the pendant;
(c) the loudspeaker;
(d) the microphone.

2 Your family has arranged for an elderly relative to have Tunstall Lifeline installed in his/her home. You have been asked to explain what it is and how it works. Write the conversation between you and your elderly relative.

Advertisements B and C

Explain clearly in your own words the similarities and the differences between the two advertisements.

Advertisements D and E

1 The two vehicles advertised have similarities and differences.
Explain what they are.

2 The advertisements also have different styles. Explain the differences and similarities (if any) in the way each sells its product.

General

1 Choose one of the advertisements. Think about how it could change the life of an elderly person. (If possible base your ideas on someone you know.) Explain how the product would change that person's life.

2 Design two advertisments for the Tunstall Lifeline. They should each be about the same size as B or D. Each should be modelled on the advertising style of one of the other advertisements. (For example, one could be modelled on B and one on C.) Try to make the contrast between the two as clear as possible.

The Miser

MISER
proves
them
wrong

Dave Starbright, landlord of the Green Man

I hardly knew him of course – I don't think anyone in the village did really. He never came in my pub. There were lots of stories about him. He used to be a farmer. Had about 200 acres over Dreinton way. Made quite a bit of money – he never spent any of it, you see. Then he took to playing the Stock Exchange. People say he made a packet buying and selling shares, but no one really *knew* how much he was worth. Then he retired to that funny old bungalow down Lower Lane. Kept himself to himself. But I think he kept on with the stocks and shares – that's what everyone said anyway. But he was a real old miser. Never spent a penny of it on anyone – even himself.

Elsie Groves, neighbour

I've lived next door to Mr Wharton for twenty years – always called him *Mr* Wharton. We never got to know him. You could go for weeks and never set eyes on him. He stayed indoors all the time, in the one room, as far as I could see. I think that was to save money on the heating. He never spent a penny on himself. All his clothes were worn out. He used to mend them himself and you could see he didn't know how to sew or anything like that. And his shoes – you should of seen his shoes. They were all holes, and do you know, he used to mend them with sellotape and bits of sticking plaster. He didn't even have a telly. The only thing he seemed to enjoy was sitting at his table – well, you could see from the garden, not that I'm nosey, or anything like that – he'd sit at his table and study all these papers — I suppose it was accounts and stocks and shares, things like that. Still it won't help him now, not where he's gone. You can't take it with you, as they say.

Wayne Jarvis, schoolboy

All the village kids were scared of him. There were all these stories about him. They said that if you went in his garden – to look for a ball or anything – he'd come out with a big stick or a knife and shout at you and chase you off. I never went in there, I was too scared. Mum and Dad say he was very rich, but I thought he looked like a poor man. His clothes were all worn out.

He left £523,500, divided up as follows:-

£190,000 to provide bungalows for three farm workers who used to work for him.

£30,000 for the upkeep of the bungalows.

£65,000 to build an extension to the village hall.

£5,000 to build a bus shelter in the village.

£2,000 for the upkeep of the churchyard.

£100,000 for the Save the Children fund.

The rest to a number of national and local charities.

Assignments

Preliminary work
You are a reporter for a local newspaper. You are preparing to write an article about the life and death of Albert Wharton, and the effects of his will. Make a set of notes about him. Use these headings:

A Known facts about his life
B His reputation in the village
C Main points about his will
D Unanswered questions (things you still need to find out)

Writing
Write the article. If you want to, invent more details, but make sure that they don't contradict the information you have been given.

Which Car?

The Domino Effect
New from Daihatsu

The Colette will take you from London to Paris and back on a tankful. In real style.

What makes the new Nissan Micra Colette such an exceptional Supermini is that not only is it light on your purse, it's also pretty as a picture and full of luxury features.

Micras have always been known for their superb equipment, such as push-button LW/MW radio, quartz clock, reclining front seats, intermittent wipers, rear wash wipe, hinged rear side windows, halogen headlights, heated rear window etc.

But the new Colette pushes luxury and value to the heights by adding luxury seat upholstery, adjustable head restraints, elegant wheel trims, a Colette badge, bodyside pin stripe and the option of two-tone paint.

All that in a car that will take you from 0-60 in 16.5 secs and yet offers fuel consumption of 56.5 mpg at cruising speed and

44.1 mpg around town. So a tankful will take you from London to Paris and back with petrol to spare. And in a car that's delightful to handle, amazingly manoeuvrable and will comfortably take four with their luggage.

And for complete peace of mind, there's that famous Nissan reliability a 6-year anti-corrosion warranty and a 3-year/100,000 mile warranty and means you can go not just from London to Paris and back but FOUR times around the world without worry. See the new Nissan Micra Colette at your dealer now.

The new Micra Colette £4699.
Other Nissan Micra models from £3999.

TWO TONE PAINT, DELIVERY, NUMBER PLATES AND ROAD FUND LICENCE EXTRA. GOVERNMENT FUEL FIGURES FOR MICRA COLETTE MPG
URBAN - 44.1 (6.4) CONSTANT 75 MPH - 42.8 (6.6). NISSAN UK LTD. NISSAN HOUSE, WORTHING, SUSSEX BN13 3HD. TEL (0903) 6856). MICRA COLETTE MPG (LITRES PER 100 KM) CONSTANT 56 MPH - 56.5 (5.0).

Building quality in Britain

NISSAN

As the most thrifty performer in town, the new Daihatsu Domino can return an impressive 70.6 mpg at 56 mph.

But this striking five door hatchback impresses in other ways too.

For a small car that comfortably accommodates four adults, it has the look and feel of a spacious saloon. Together with features that would embarrass some of those in the luxury class.

And with all this at just £3,995;** clearly the Domino knocks spots off its rivals.

For more information simply fill in the coupon or dial 100 and ask for Freefone 9507. Or pop along to your local dealer and experience the Domino Effect for yourself.

*Govt. fuel figs: 48.7 mpg (5.8l/100 km) Urban, 70.6 mpg (4l/100 km) at 56 mph, 44.8 mpg (6.3l/100 km) at 75 mph. **Price correct at time of going to press. Inc. VAT and car tax. Exc. delivery, road tax and no. plates

The most economical petrol car in Britain

Send to: Daihatsu (UK) Ltd., Freepost, P.O. Box 5, Dover CT17 0BR. (No stamp required.)

Name _____

Address _____   W/16/A

Postcode _____ Tel No. _____

DAIHATSU
DOMINO

More choice
Look over the new Fiat Pandas and you'll find a few changes; a sleeker, tidier body on all four models, and a brand new 750cc Panda built to combine lively performance with low cost and economy, yet offering the proven practicality of all Pandas.
Drive any of the new Pandas and you'll feel a world of difference. Because for 1986 we've added fresh muscle to elegance, with new power.

economy, handling and comfort.
New FIRE
Beneath every Panda's bonnet lives a new Fully Integrated Robotized Engine (FIRE) built to add fire to Panda's performance with greater pulling power and much reduced need for maintenance.
More for your comfort
Inside there's a new dashboard and instruments – more luxurious

seats front and rear, with rear access improved by front seats that tilt and slide.
Better ride and handling
Out on the road there's new comfort too, thanks to 'Omega' rear suspension offering pin sharp handling and a more compliant ride.
Outstanding economy
With 56.6 mpg† at 56 mph from the Panda 750L and 1000CL and

an outstanding 61.4 mpg† from the 1000 Super, Panda economy's never looked healthier.
All thanks to the new FIRE.
Some things, though, we'll never change: Panda's unique versatility, its high load carrying capacity, and of course its unrivalled value for money.
Because, new muscle and all, the new Panda range now weighs in at just £3,290†† fighting fit and ready for anything.

NEW PANDA FIRE

90": 1000 CL £3599": 1000 SUPER £3939": 4x4 £4872."

MORE MUSCLE WHERE IT MATTERS. MORE FIRE IN ITS BELLY.

FIAT
SETTING NEW STANDARDS

61

THE SUPERMINI OF TODAY
NIPPY · PRACTICAL · FUN · INEXPENSIVE

Put any Yugo through its paces and you'll soon discover you're driving one of the best all-rounders on the road today.

Take it to town and you've got a versatile performer. Nippy in traffic. Easy to park.

On the open road the Yugo hatchbacks are just as much fun to drive.

A responsive engine helping you to cruise effortlessly along the motorway and conserve petrol (47 mpg at a constant 56 mph†).

Less compromising country roads leave the Yugo unshaken too.

With positive front wheel drive and light and precise rack and pinion steering helping you round the sharpest of bends.

Sturdy all-round independent suspension soaking up the most punishing of potholes. And dependable dual circuit brakes stopping you safely every time.

Passengers too will enjoy the ride. Four adults can travel in complete comfort.

And still find plenty of room for their luggage.

You can see the most affordable hatchbacks in Britain today at any of the Yugo dealers listed here. Today.

The Yugo Range from only £2999*

Assignments

All these advertisements are for cars that are, relatively, inexpensive to buy and economical to run. Nevertheless, although the products are similar, they are advertised in very different ways.

Preliminary work

For each advertisement, make a list of the following information (where available):

1 Your initial response to the advertisement
2 The exact name of the car(s) being advertised
3 Petrol consumption
4 Top speed and information about performance
5 Roadholding and steering
6 Driving controls and instruments
7 Interior arrangements and comfort
8 Luggage capacity
9 Servicing
10 Any other selling points
11 The visual approach used in the advertisement — what it *looks* like
12 Key words used in the advertisement — what it *sounds* like

Commenting on the advertisements

Comment on the content and style of the advertisements, explaining which you think is the most effective and which is the least effective and why.

Designing an advertisement

Choose the advertisement which you think is the least effective. Imagine that you have been given the job of improving it.
Either:
(a) design a new advertisement for the same car;
or:
(b) write a detailed set of instructions for the advertising agency explaining what is wrong with the present advertisement and how you want it changed.

Our On-the-Spot Reporter ...

Assignments

Questions to think about

1 What has happened?
2 What is the reporter trying to do?
3 Why does the man attack him?
4 What does the man do then?
5 Why does he do that?
6 What is the point of the small row of pictures along the bottom of the cartoon?
7 What is the point of the cartoon as a whole?
8 Do you agree with it?

Writing

1 Look at the small row of pictures along the top of the cartoon.
 Make up words to go in each of the speech balloons.
2 Many people would agree with the point the cartoonist is making.
 Write a letter of complaint from such a person to either the BBC or the IBA.
3 Imagine that the cartoonist meets a reporter like Jon Pollitt.
 They have an argument. Write the script of what is said.

Train Crash

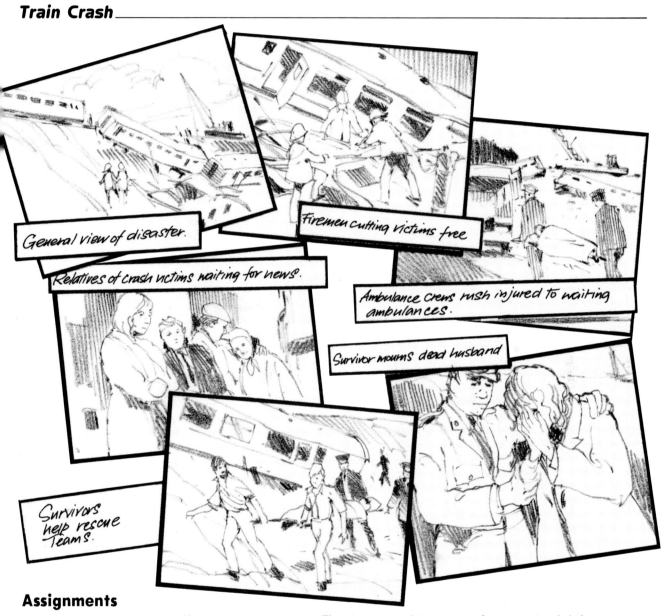

General view of disaster.

Firemen cutting victims free

Relatives of crash victims waiting for news.

Ambulance crews rush injured to waiting ambulances.

Survivor mourns dead husband

Survivors help rescue Teams.

Assignments

You are a news reporter. The pictures on this page are from a national daily newspaper. You have been given the job of interviewing people involved and writing a detailed report.

1 Make a list of people you would try to interview.
2 Make a list of the questions you would ask each one.
3 Write the script of *one* of the interviews.
4 Write your news report — if possible in the style of a particular newspaper.
5 Suppose that this event were reported on BBC news or on ITN. Write a script of how it might be presented.

Leroy Is Missing!

Leroy _____

When things happened

0800	Leroy has breakfast with family as normal
0835	Leroy's usual bus arrives outside school, but Leroy isn't on it
0855	Leroy is marked absent on class register
1820	Leroy's mother rings one of Leroy's teachers
1850	Teacher rings back to tell her that Leroy hasn't been in school all day
1905	Leroy's mother rings the police

Statement by James Flynn

'I saw him at the bus stop on my way to school. It must have been just after quarter past eight. I was on my bike and he was standing looking at the bus timetable. I often see him there in the morning. I shouted to him and waved but he didn't even look up. I thought that was a bit strange, because he always gives me a wave as I go by.'

Part of the mother's statement to the police

'He left home at the usual time – about ten past eight. He seemed all right – a bit quiet, perhaps, but nothing out of the ordinary. He usually catches the bus to school at about twenty past eight. Then he gets home again at about quarter past four. When it got round to half past five I began to wonder what had happened to him. You see it's not like him to come in late without letting us know. He's always been such a good reliable boy ... No, I don't think he's in any sort of trouble. He always seems to be getting on so well at school. All the teachers like him ...'

Statement by Mr Winston Hughes, a friend of Leroy's father

'Yes, I saw the boy. He was at the railway station – just standing there, in the entrance, looking at the timetable of trains to Manchester. I thought it was rather unusual, because it was late – the time must have been about quarter to nine – and he should have been at school by then. I said, 'Hello, Leroy, what are you doing here?' and he looked very embarrassed. Then he just muttered something about being on his way to school ...'

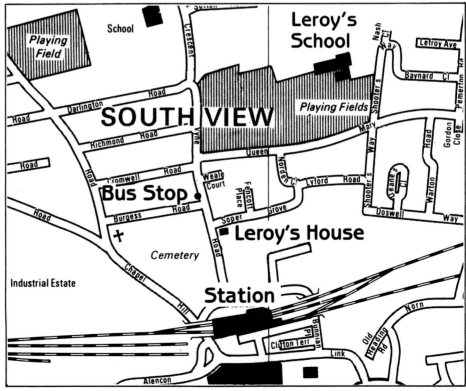

Assignments

Preliminary work

1 Copy and complete the table of 'When things happened'.
2 What evidence is there that Leroy
   (a) was behaving normally that morning?
   (b) was not behaving normally that morning?
3 What evidence is there that Leroy was not telling Mr Hughes the truth when he said that he was on his way to school?

Writing

1 Write a 'missing person' description of Leroy.
2 Write a report for the local newspaper describing the events of Leroy's disappearance.

School _____

Leroy's last report

English: Leroy has a lively imagination but unfortunately this doesn't always show in his writing which is often careless and hurried.
        W.S.

Mathematics: Still finding difficulties which are not helped by carelessness and inattention
        AE.

French: He has clearly given up all hope in this subject and is just wasting his time
        ME

Geography: Leroy is continuing to make good progress and should do well in his exams
        LM

History: His work is very erratic. Sometimes it is of a good standard, but it can be careless
        SP.

Technical Drawing: Leroy works very hard and is beginning to get really good results. He is prepared to take considerable trouble to get it right.
        PP.

Metalwork: Improving all the time. Very good application and attention to detail
        HM.

P.E.: Excellent work in athletics representing school, District and County Under-16's
        SC.

House Tutor: It is almost as if there are two Leroys — one careful and hardworking; the other slapdash e careless. There is still time for Leroy to do something about this before the exams, but only if he acts _now_
        J.S.

Statement by Mr A. Edgeworth, Leroy's maths teacher

'I have taught Leroy for the last year and a half. He is in the bottom set for maths, although I think he is not unintelligent. The trouble is he will not pay attention when a topic is being explained. As a result, when it comes to doing the exercises he doesn't know what he's supposed to be doing. So he just sits there and fools around with his friends until I tell him off or give him some extra work. He's not a bad boy, he's just completely given up where maths is concerned – and it's not as if he's stupid. If he gave a quarter the thought to his maths he did to thinking up excuses to explain why he hasn't done his homework, he'd be top of the class.'

Statement by Mrs W. Symonds, Leroy's English teacher

'He's not all that good at English, because he isn't prepared to take the trouble, but he's lively and imaginative. He's very good orally, because he's interested in so many different things. And he really cares about things. But he's inclined to be rather moody – I think that explains why his school reports are so uneven. If he takes against a particular teacher, then that's it – he won't do any work in that subject. He's a very caring boy in lots of ways. For instance, we've started a social service unit that meets after school and finds useful work to do to help the community, and he's a leading light in that. But just recently he's seemed rather withdrawn – as if he's having one of his 'down' phases – but it's lasted a good bit longer than they usually do.'

Assignments

Preliminary work
1 What is the evidence in Leroy's report to back up what his house tutor says?
2 What impression do you get of the personalities of Mr Edgeworth and Mrs Symonds? What are the reasons for this?
3 Is there anything on these two pages to suggest why Leroy has disappeared?
4 Think of all the possible things that could have happened to Leroy and make a list of them.

Writing
1 Mr Edgeworth and Mrs Symonds discuss Leroy's school career with the Headmaster. Write the conversation they have.
2 The Headmaster is asked by the police to make a confidential report on Leroy. Write that report.
3 Decide for yourself where you think Leroy went and why. Then write an account of 'What happened to Leroy', as if you were him. (Write as 'I'.)

Volcano

Thousands die in Columbia

At least fifteen thousand people and possibly as many as fifty thousand are now feared to have died in Colombia following the eruption on Wednesday of the volcano Nevada del Ruiz. Most of them perished when a river, blocked by volcanic debris, finally burst through the wall of mud engulfing the prosperous town of Armero in the middle of Colombia's main coffee-growing area. The twenty-three thousand inhabitants had virtually no chance of escape. Although more than nine hundred people have been rescued from the town, many were buried by the avalanche and others are surviving on patches of high ground or even in the branches of trees. An international relief operation has begun, including American planes with emergency supplies from Panama. The British Embassy has sent a list of desperately needed items to London, including antibiotics, blood plasma and clothing, but the situation is still confused and, as Brian Barron now reports from Bogota, the catastrophe is far from over. . . . .

'Even as rescuers were dragging the dead and the living from the tidal wave of mud that engulfed the Armero valley, fresh tremors from the volcano shook the region. The relief operation is being hampered by the collapse of bridges and the flooding of roads everywhere, and Red Cross workers at the scene say flood waters are still rising. There's no precise death toll yet but early today an official spokesman said fifteen thousand people are missing in Armero. The assumption is: most are dead, buried beneath a wall of mud up to twenty feet high. So far the main rescue operation is being done by Colombian army helicopters, though rain for the third day running is restricting flights. It's clear now that several weeks ago the coffee growers and town residents of the Armero valley were advised to leave by government engineers but most chose to ignore those warnings, refusing to abandon their crops, having no money and no other homes to go to.'

BBC Radio 4 News, 15 November 1985

20,000 DEAD
Entire town wiped out by volcano

About 20,000 people died in their beds yesterday as a volcano engulfed their town.

Homes vanished under a 15ft wall of mud and ash from the ferocious pre-dawn eruption.

And a pilot flying over Armero, in Colombia, South America, where 50,000 people had lived, reported: 'It's fearsome. There's nothing left.'

The snow-capped 16,000ft Nevada del Ruiz mountain had been sleeping for nearly 400 years since its last major blast in 1595. Experts had warned it was beginning to wake – but too late to save families who refused to leave their houses and crops.

A nearby river burst its banks, sending floodwater crashing into the town as survivors tried to flee.

Trucks packed with people were swept away, and rescue workers later saw dismembered bodies floating downstream in water turned yellow with sulphur. ➡

One worker said: 'It is easier to count the living than the dead. The panorama is desolate. It looks like a nuclear bomb has exploded.' Survivor Jose Gaitan wept as he described the horror. 'Ashes began covering the houses,' he said.

'We heard the roar of the river and we took off on foot. A lot of people tried to leave on motorcycles or cars but they couldn't because of the mud.

'We tried to reach the hills but it was impossible. Many of my relatives are missing.'

Red Cross director Artemo Franco said: 'Rescue workers are talking about 20,000 dead and 25,000 injured. It is an immense tragedy.' 'Eighty-five per cent of the town is destroyed,' local state governor Eduardo Alzate confirmed.

Another pilot who was flying past at the time of the eruption said: 'I saw a great orange flash, then was surrounded by smoke and had trouble controlling the plane.'

SURVIVORS

Helicopters were being used to reach survivors who had climbed trees and were waving for help.

Rescue work was hampered by the remoteness of the town, high in the Andes mountains.

*The world's worst death toll from a volcano was in Indonesia in 1815 when Mount Tambora erupted, killing more than 92,000 people.

Sun, 15 November 1985

20,000 DEAD AS VOLCANO ERUPTS

At least 20,000 people were feared dead yesterday after a volcano 'exploded like a bomb'.

The volcano, in the Andes Mountains, west of Bogota, Columbia, erupted twice, showering the area with molten lava and causing massive landslides and flooding.

The town of Armero, with a population of 25,000, was completely buried by 15ft of mud and ash.

The white-hot lava melted the permanent snow on the mountainsides, causing massive flooding and mud slides.

Heavy rains, which have pounded the remote coffee-growing area for three days, added to the horror.

SMOKE

Large parts of four other towns were washed away by rivers of water and mud.

Rescue workers were hampered by the torrential rain and vast clouds of smoke and ash from the volcano, which had lain dormant for nearly 400 years.

A pilot who flew over Armero, 100 miles north-west of Bogota, said: 'The town has disappeared.

'What is left looks like a desert or a beach.'

The volcano, called Nevado del Ruiz, which last erupted in 1595, began sending sinister columns of smoke into the area three months ago.

Despite the fears of the area's inhabitants, geologists told them the volcano was likely to remain dormant.

During Wednesday night it erupted twice.

One observer said: 'It exploded like a bomb, shooting lava, ashes and smoke miles into the air.

'It was like a vision of Hell.'

Mirror, Friday 15 November 1985

Assignments

Comparing the different versions

1 Copy and complete this table:

	BBC	Sun	Mirror
Population of Armero			
Number rescued			
Number missing/feared dead			
Name of volcano			
Height of volcano			
Height of wall of mud			
Were local people warned?			
What the devastated area looked like			
Other useful and relevant information			

2 Write a paragraph comparing the amount and quality of information given by each news item.

3 What would you say about the *style* of each item? Write at least one separate sentence about each and back up what you say by a short quotation.

4 Compare the way in which the news of the volcano disaster is presented on the front pages of the *Sun*, the *Mirror* and *The Times*.

Your writing
The list of facts below represents what actually happened in an accident at sea. Use them to write two different news reports of the event:

(a) as given by BBC Radio 4;
(b) as given by the *Sun* or the *Mirror*.

Make up any other information and quotations you need.

Facts:
(1) Incident happened at Brighton
(2) Wind Force 8 (Gale Force) blowing
(3) Pleasure boat, the *Merry Maid*, taking holidaymakers along coast
(4) Boat blown on to pier end
(5) Hole in side, above and below water line
(6) Rapidly filled with water and began to sink
(7) 126 people on board plus crew of 3
(8) 32 people scrambled on to pier
(9) Rest jumped into sea
(10) 15 injured, 3 seriously
(11) 2 (elderly couple) still missing.
(12) Holidaymakers and local people jumped into sea to help with rescue

Streetcrime

'How safe do you feel walking alone in your area after dark?'

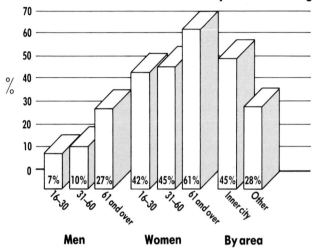

Men			Women			By area	
7%	10%	27%	42%	45%	61%	45%	28%
16-30	31-60	61 and over	16-30	31-60	61 and over	Inner city	Other

Percentage of those questioned who said that they felt 'a bit' or 'very' unsafe.

Actual mugging rates % classified as victims

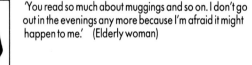

Men			Women			By area		
0.9%	0.4%	0.1%	0.6%	0.4%	0.2%	1.3%	0.5%	0.2%
16-30	31-60	61 and over	16-30	31-60	61 and over	Inner city	Other urban areas	Rural

This block chart shows the percentage of those questioned who had actually been the victims of mugging attacks.

'The fear of something happening to me does affect my life. I really don't like going out alone after dark and if I do, I'm always looking over my shoulder.' (Young woman)

'I don't worry for myself but I gave my daughter an alarm and tell her to phone for me to collect her if she can't get home.' (Father)

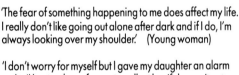

'You read so much about muggings and so on. I don't go out in the evenings any more because I'm afraid it might happen to me.' (Elderly woman)

Increase your safety

There are no hard-and-fast rules for what to do if you are attacked; how you react will depend on the situation and on your personality. But you can take certain common-sense precautions to reduce your chances of being a victim.

1 If you know you're going to be out late, think about how you'll get home beforehand, and carry enough money for a taxi just in case.
2 Walk quickly, and look confident.
3 Walk facing traffic, in the middle of the pavement. Avoid dimly lit short cuts.
4 Have your keys ready when approaching your home or car.
5 If you think you're being followed, cross the road and change your pace to see if the person behind sticks with you. If they do, move to where you know there will be more people (a pub or busy street, say) and ask for help. Failing that, go to the nearest lit house and knock on the door. →

6 Don't have jewellery obviously on show. Gold chains, for example, can be pulled from people's necks.

7 Carry your handbag close to your body - don't let it swing loose from your shoulder. Keep it shut, and don't leave your purse on top of a shopping bag or open handbag. Don't carry a wallet in your back pocket.

8 Carry your keys on your person, so that if your bag is stolen the thief won't have your keys and your address. Should this happen, change your locks.

9 Avoid empty train compartments and sit downstairs on empty buses.
If possible, sit near the guard, conductor, or driver.
If you see or hear someone screaming or asking for help, DON'T ignore them. Either intervene yourself or get others to help you.
Rushing off to call the police is better than nothing.

Can you hit back?

The law says you can protect yourself, but that you may use 'no more force than is necessary for mere defence. If an assault is threatened, a person may use such force as is reasonable in the circumstances to repel it.'

If someone attacked you and you managed to get him on the ground and run away, that would be self-defence and 'reasonable'. If you got him on the ground, then kicked and beat him when you could have escaped, that would not be reasonable and you could be prosecuted for assault.

It is an offence to carry a weapon that is obviously designed or adapted to cause injury – a cosh or knuckleduster, say – 'without lawful authority or reasonable excuse'. *You* would have to prove you had a good reason.

But what would happen if you carried something that wasn't actually an offensive weapon in its own right – pepper, or a pair of scissors, perhaps? In this case, it would be up to the *prosecution* to prove you had carried it with the intention of injuring someone, before you could be convicted of carrying an offensive weapon. For example, a carpenter was on his way home from work, carrying his tools in a case. He quarrelled with another passenger as they tried to board a tube train and he got out a hammer and hit the man with it. Though convicted of assault, he was not found guilty of carrying an offensive weapon because there was no evidence that he had carried the hammer with the intention of using it to cause injury.

'Self-defence' would not be a reasonable excuse for carrying an offensive weapon, unless there was a particular and imminent threat to you. A taxi driver who carried a cosh in his cab for self-defence, for example, and argued that taxi drivers were sometimes attacked at night, was found guilty of carrying an offensive weapon because there was only the off-chance of an attack.

Which?, November 1985

Assignments

The risks

1 Who is most likely to feel unsafe walking alone after dark? Write a paragraph explaining what the bar chart shows.
2 Who is most likely to be attacked?
3 Compare your answers to (1) and (2). Why do you think there are these differences?
4 Write a conversation between an elderly woman and a police officer who knows the figures and is trying to reassure her.

Self-defence and the law

5 Read 'Increase your safety' and 'Can you hit back? on pages 75 and 76
   Comment on this picture story:

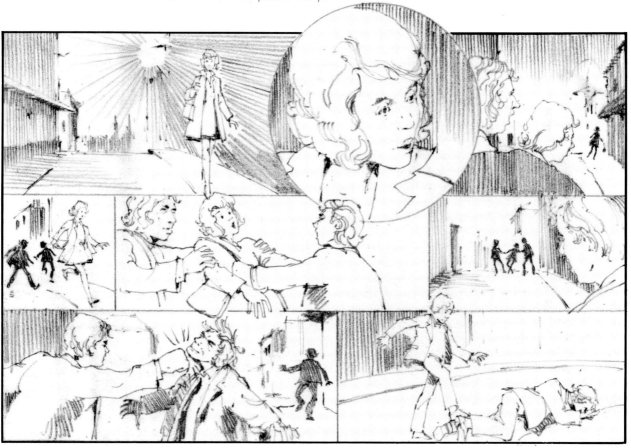

6 Is each of these people right or wrong, and why?

I always carry a spanner in the cab in case I get attacked. The police can't do me for that - it's self defence.

These days if someone attacks you, you can't even defend yourself without being charged with assault.

This bloke attacked me and I knocked him over and ran away. He banged his head and now they're doing me for assault. It was only self defence.

Giveaway

Make us millionaires, Mr Taxman

Section A

1 Hooray for Mrs Sainsbury, who after a lifetime of explaining that no, she's not related to the food store, has made her own name by giving a cool million to Covent Garden. I'm delighted, not just because slightly fewer flakes of plaster may now float down into the open mouths of the singers, but because it's exhilarating to think that anyone can pick up a vast chunk of money and simply give it away.

2 I feel the same about Eugene Lang, an American millionaire who five years ago was about to make a speech to sixth-graders in Harlem; he looked at them, tore up his speech (no doubt an act of generosity in itself) and said simply: 'Don't drop out. If you take your exams I'll pay your way through college' – and 52 out of the 61 have stuck with it.

3 I feel that way about a friend who, not believing in inherited wealth, put practically all of his into a charitable trust; or the woman who walked into the Dutch Embassy after the disastrous floods of 1953 and said 'Here's the money I was going to spend on a holiday in Holland – give it to the relief fund'. Or an uncle of mine who was visiting a hard-up couple in a remote part of Scotland, who spend their entire time helping other people (I'd say social work only it sounds so statutory). They were desperate because their ancient car had finally died on them. 'You'd better have mine,' said the uncle, 'I don't drive much these days' – and back he went to Berkshire by British Rail.

4 It's so heartening when anyone shows they *don't* put money first; such a welcome counterblast to our current money morality. This warped distortion of economics starts by saying that most people probably *will* follow their own best financial interest, and then somehow goes on to imply that they *should*. This is not the far-sighted common sense that made nurturing real land with real trees and fields a virtue; it's simply what the Greeks called scornfully 'the making of more'; where the ideal is not being better – just better off.

Section B

1 You'd think that the more money you had, the easier it would be to throw it about, but it doesn't seem to be so. You'd think the richest man in America would have some fun with his money; yet there is Sam Walton in all the newspapers priding himself on his modest lifestyle. I find that extraordinary: if you don't want to spend the money, why not give it all away to someone who does?

2 When you or I dream about being millionaires, one of the best fantasies is the giving: the swimming-pool you could build for the village, the shivering granny you could centrally heat, the school you could endow for musical children; in my teens I even dreamed of starting a co-operative laundry, though I can't now remember why.

3 But as soon as you formulate such plans, the snag becomes apparent. Is the pool to be covered or open? Should it be gas central heating or electricity, and what happens if granny wants to sell up? What kind of music are the kids to learn in school – *and who decides*?

4 As soon as you use money, you use – or are in a position to use – power. And that is a very different thing, if only because people will then try to take it away from you. I presume that's why the big givers do it through foundations and trusts, but that can be no fun at all, compared to giving a fiver to some grimy-faced children to blow themselves up with their guy.

5 I know why the idea of private giving fell into such disrepute: it seemed too easy a way of feeling virtuous, and since no one would ever give a fraction of what's taken in tax, there would never in a million years be enough of it for all that's needed. In the nineteenth century when public medicine and social welfare depended on private charity people were far worse off than they are now. And though giving may be great for the giver, it's still tough that the recipients have to feel grateful.

Section C

1 But experience does suggest that we may have underestimated the attraction of a true, spontaneous handing over of what you have to someone who needs it more. If I were the government, I'd be tempted to encourage it: to let everybody have one lump of their tax to lay out as they pleased. Then Miss Flower could plant primroses on Primrose Hill, Sir Thingummy Pencil endow an owl sanctuary; one man could give books to a library, another build a bus shelter; some soft-hearted auntie could cause chockies to rain down on a primary school as to the manna born.

2 It would certainly be more fun than just paying taxes; and make us all feel for a moment like millionaires.

Katharine Whitehorn, *Observer*, 27 October 1985

Where the Money Goes

How an overseas charity might spend it	£
1 month's salary of a village health worker in Gujarat	3
A piece of plastic sheeting to provide emergency shelter for a family in Calcutta when fire destroyed 40 huts	5
A rake, a bucket and a watering can for a vegetable growing project in Senegal	11
A handsaw for a carpentry and housebuilding project in a Miskito Indian community in Nicaragua	16
A vaccine carrier incorporating an ice pack in rural Zaire	20

Figures from *Oxfam*, January 1986

Charity Giving

Donations to charities in 1984
In millions of pounds

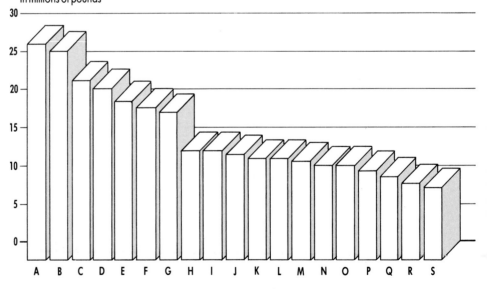

A Oxfam
B National Trust
C Royal National Lifeboat Institution
D Cancer Research Campaign
E Imperial Cancer Research Fund
F Salvation Army
G Dr Barnado's
H Save the Children Fund
I National Society for the Prevention of Cruelty to Children

J Help the Aged
K Royal National Institute for the Blind
L Spastic Society
M Guide Dogs for the Blind Association
N Christian Aid
O Action Aid
P Jewish Philanthropic Association
Q Marie Curie Memorial Foundation
R Royal British Legion
S Church of England Children's Society

Assignments

Make us millionaires, Mr Taxman

Section A
1. What does the writer approve of about the people she describes in paragraphs 1—3?
2. What does she say in paragraph 4 she disapproves of?

Section B
3. In paragraph 2 she describes one of the 'best fantasies' about being a millionaire and in paragraph 3 she outlines 'the snag'. Explain what they are.
4. 'I know why the idea of private giving fell into such disrepute.' Why?

Section C
5. Explain in your own words the plan she outlines in this section.

Writing
1. Comment on (a) the arguments and (b) the plan contained in Katharine Whitehorn's article.
2. Write an argument between these two people:

A believes

Charity begins at home
You shouldn't have to rely on the Government
People should have more control over their own money to spend according to their consciences
People *are* generous

B believes

If it was left to people's consciences those in need would suffer
Individual people don't have enough information about who really *is* in need
If people paid fewer taxes, many would just keep the rest for themselves

Where the money goes
Use the information provided to compose an advertisement for a charity. One way to do this would be to compare the ways in which the charity uses the money with those in which a reasonably affluent person might spend the same amount on himself or herself.

Charity giving
1. Imagine that these figures have just been released. Write a paragraph for a newspaper under the headline 'Britain's Top Charities'.
2. If you had £1,000 to give away, how would you divide it up? Present your answer in two ways:
   (a) as a block chart showing how much money is given to each charity;
   (b) as a piece of writing explaining how and why you have allocated the money in this way.

Cycling

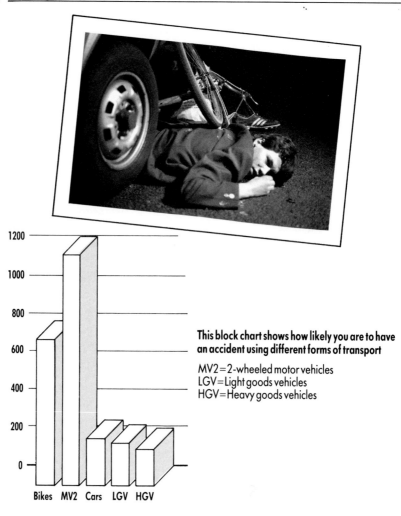

This block chart shows how likely you are to have an accident using different forms of transport

MV2 = 2-wheeled motor vehicles
LGV = Light goods vehicles
HGV = Heavy goods vehicles

Killed or seriously injured in road accidents 1983

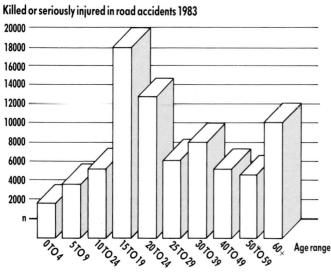

Vehicles involved in road accidents 1973–1983

1973 1974 1975 1976 1977 1978 1979 1980 1981 1982 1983

Motor vehicles of all types

Pedal cycles (% increase 1973-1983 = 53.7%)

1973 1974 1975 1976 1977 1978 1979 1980 1981 1982 1983

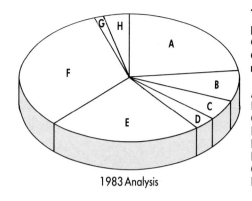

This pie chart shows the percentages of people killed or seriously injured in traffic accidents according to the means of transport

A	Pedestrian	24%
B	Cycle	6%
C	Moped	4%
D	Motor scooters	2%
E	Motorcycles	24%
F	Car	35%
G	Bus	1%
H	Lorry	3%

1983 Analysis

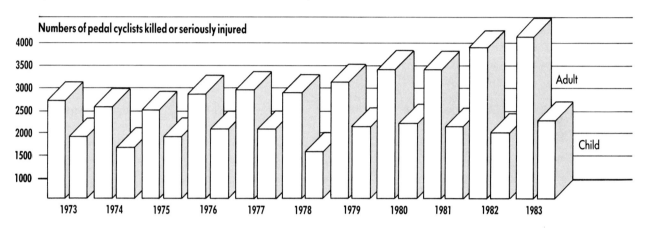

Assignments

Questions

1   What is the evidence that cycling is a dangerous form of transport, compared with other means of travel?

2   Is there any evidence to the contrary?

3   What are the arguments for and against the belief that child cyclists are at risk?

Writing

1   You are a road safety officer. Study the information on this page. You have the funds to run one special safety campaign this year. Write a report for your boss explaining to him:
(a)   what that campaign will be;
(b)   your reasons for it.

2   Write an argument between a motorist and a cyclist about which form of transport is the most dangerous. Use the information provided to back up the two arguments.

3   Use the information as the basis for a newspaper report with the headline 'Danger on the Roads'.

Every year thousands of junior school children take the National Cycling Proficiency Test. The tester has a detailed marksheet and watches the child do a variety of different manoeuvres.

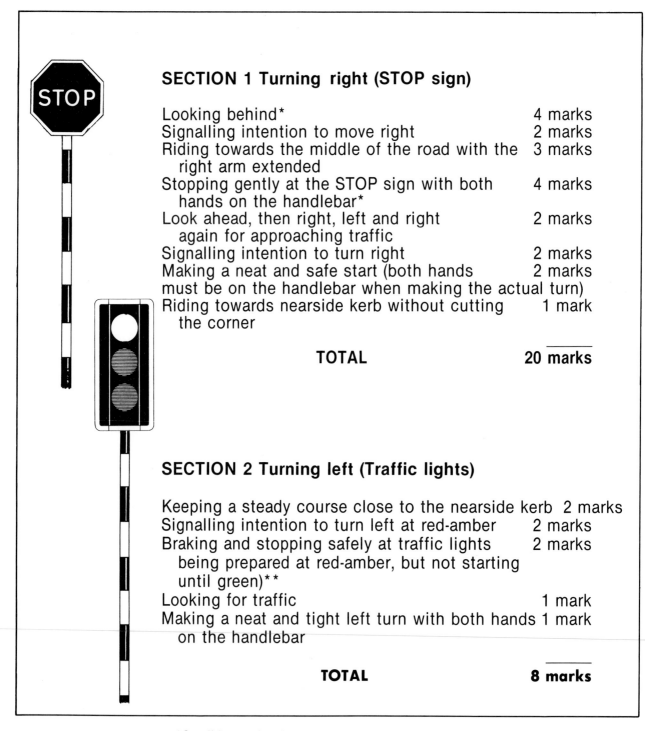

SECTION 1 Turning right (STOP sign)

Looking behind*	4 marks
Signalling intention to move right	2 marks
Riding towards the middle of the road with the right arm extended	3 marks
Stopping gently at the STOP sign with both hands on the handlebar*	4 marks
Look ahead, then right, left and right again for approaching traffic	2 marks
Signalling intention to turn right	2 marks
Making a neat and safe start (both hands must be on the handlebar when making the actual turn)	2 marks
Riding towards nearside kerb without cutting the corner	1 mark
TOTAL	**20 marks**

SECTION 2 Turning left (Traffic lights)

Keeping a steady course close to the nearside kerb	2 marks
Signalling intention to turn left at red-amber	2 marks
Braking and stopping safely at traffic lights being prepared at red-amber, but not starting until green)**	2 marks
Looking for traffic	1 mark
Making a neat and tight left turn with both hands on the handlebar	1 mark
TOTAL	**8 marks**

*Candidates who do not stop at the line, or do not look behind where the tests require that they shall do so, must be failed.

SECTION 1 Turning right   **SECTION 2 Turning left**

Assignments

1 For each section of the test opposite give the children above the mark you think s/he has gained.

2 Write a brief report on the child's performance in the two sections.

On Location

Independent Broadcasting Company
Merchant Street
Birmingham B43 RT7

The Headmaster,
St. Peter's High School,
Dean's Court,
Starbridge.

23rd January, 1987

Dear Mr. Hadland,

Following our recent conversation, I am writing formally to request your co-operation in the use of your school as a location for our forthcoming drama production Rebels and Losers.

As I explained when we met, we are making a serial based on life in a modern comprehensive school and we want to make it as realistic as possible. We want to do some of our filming in a real school, and to use real children in a number of scenes. Your school seems to have just the right setting, and the right atmosphere, for our purposes.

Please let me know whether there is any more information you need about the project.

Yours sincerely,

A. Worpole

Arthur Worpole,
Drama Producer

St. Peter's High School
Dean's Court
Starbridge

Mr A. Worpole,
Independent Broadcasting Company,
Merchant Street,
Birmingham, B43 RT7

3rd February 1987

Dear Mr Worpole,

Thank you for your letter about your plans to use our school as a location for a TV drama series. I have discussed this matter with the School Governors and we see no reason in principle why this should not be possible.

There are, however, a number of points on which we should like further information. Most of them can be cleared up on the phone, but there are two questions to which I should like an answer in writing.

1   What is the story which you propose to film - is there anything in it which is likely to harm the reputation of the school?

2   When we talked, you mentioned some financial recompense to the school because of the disruption caused. I should be grateful if you would tell me approximately how much this is likely to be. (I am going to have to sell this idea to the teachers at my school and this information would certainly help.)

I look forward to hearing from you.

Yours sincerely,

D.K. Hadland.

D.K. Hadland, Headmaster.

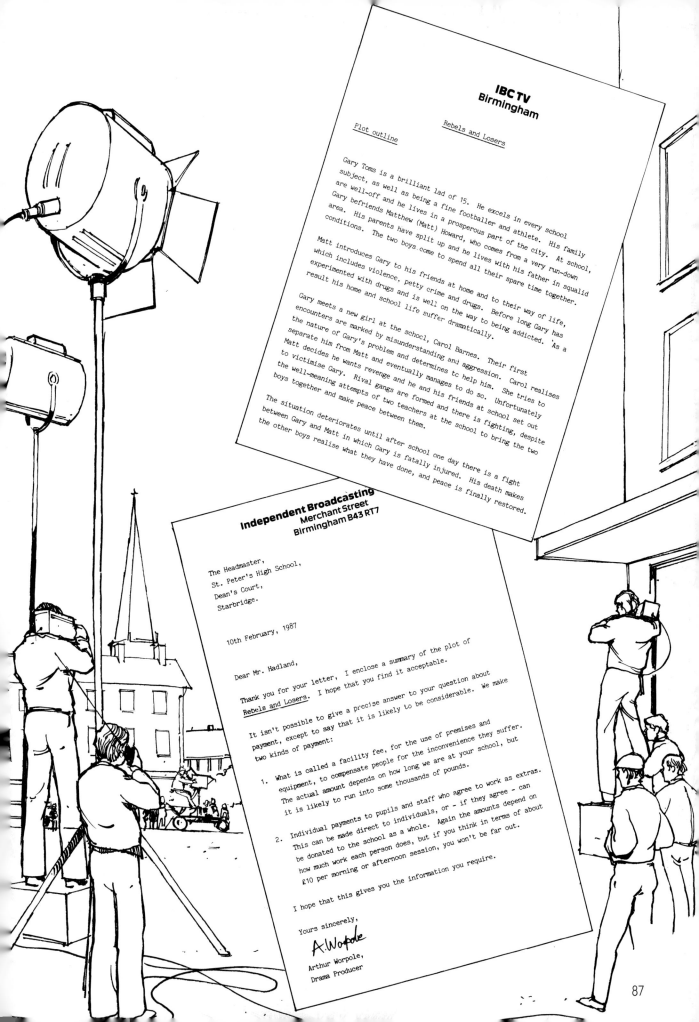

IBC TV
Birmingham

Plot outline   Rebels and Losers

Gary Toms is a brilliant lad of 15. He excels in every school subject, as well as being a fine footballer and athlete. His family are well-off and he lives in a prosperous part of the city. At school, Gary befriends Matthew (Matt) Howard, who comes from a very run-down area. His parents have split up and he lives with his father in squalid conditions. The two boys come to spend all their spare time together.

Matt introduces Gary to his friends at home and to their way of life, which includes violence, petty crime and drugs. Before long Gary has experimented with drugs and is well on the way to being addicted. As a result his home and school life suffer dramatically.

Gary meets a new girl at the school, Carol Barnes. Their first encounters are marked by misunderstanding and aggression. Carol realises the nature of Gary's problem and determines to help him. She tries to separate him from Matt and eventually manages to do so. Unfortunately Matt decides he wants revenge and he and his friends at school set out to victimise Gary. Rival gangs are formed and there is fighting, despite the well-meaning attempts of two teachers at the school to bring the two boys together and make peace between them.

The situation deteriorates until after school one day there is a fight between Gary and Matt in which Gary is fatally injured. His death makes the other boys realise what they have done, and peace is finally restored.

Independent Broadcasting
Merchant Street
Birmingham B43 RT7

The Headmaster,
St. Peter's High School,
Dean's Court,
Starbridge.

10th February, 1987

Dear Mr. Hadland,

Thank you for your letter, I enclose a summary of the plot of Rebels and Losers. I hope that you find it acceptable.

It isn't possible to give a precise answer to your question about payment, except to say that it is likely to be considerable. We make two kinds of payment:

1. What is called a facility fee, for the use of premises and equipment, to compensate people for the inconvenience they suffer. The actual amount depends on how long we are at your school, but it is likely to run into some thousands of pounds.

2. Individual payments to pupils and staff who agree to work as extras. This can be made direct to individuals, or - if they agree - can be donated to the school as a whole. Again the amounts depend on how much work each person does, but if you think in terms of about £10 per morning or afternoon session, you won't be far out.

I hope that this gives you the information you require.

Yours sincerely,

A.Worpole

Arthur Worpole,
Drama Producer

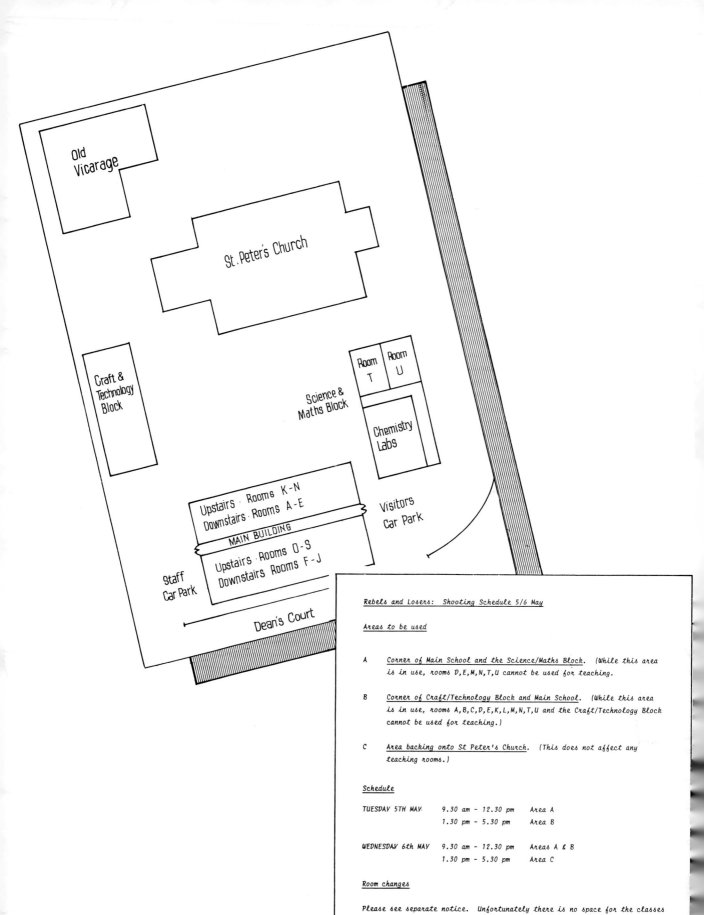

Old Vicarage

St. Peter's Church

Craft & Technology Block

Science & Maths Block

Room T Room U

Chemistry Labs

Upstairs · Rooms K-N
Downstairs · Rooms A-E

MAIN BUILDING

Upstairs · Rooms O-S
Downstairs · Rooms F-J

Visitors Car Park

Staff Car Park

Dean's Court

Rebels and Losers: Shooting Schedule 5/6 May

Areas to be used

A   Corner of Main School and the Science/Maths Block. (While this area
    is in use, rooms D,E,M,N,T,U cannot be used for teaching.

B   Corner of Craft/Technology Block and Main School. (While this area
    is in use, rooms A,B,C,D,E,K,L,M,N,T,U and the Craft/Technology Block
    cannot be used for teaching.)

C   Area backing onto St Peter's Church. (This does not affect any
    teaching rooms.)

Schedule

TUESDAY 5TH MAY   9.30 am – 12.30 pm   Area A
                   1.30 pm – 5.30 pm   Area B

WEDNESDAY 6th MAY 9.30 am – 12.30 pm   Areas A & B
                   1.30 pm – 5.30 pm   Area C

Room changes

Please see separate notice. Unfortunately there is no space for the classes
normally in rooms T and U. They will have to do private study in the library.

Location Unit

From : Jennie Tyson, Location Manager, Rebels and Losers

Date : Monday 27th April

Dear Ms Pearce,

Thank you for your letter. We'd be very happy for you to bring your 4th year English class to watch the filming on Wednesday afternoon. We shall be working on a sequence in which a fight breaks out between boys from the rival gangs. We shall begin by explaining to the boys who are extras what they have to do. Then we shall rehearse their part in the scene. After that the principal actors will join us and we'll rehearse the scene with them. When we are happy with the rehearsal, we'll have our first take. I suggest that at that stage, small groups of your pupils can watch from the mobile control room. In this way, they should all get a chance to see how the director controls the shooting. We'll finish by showing the class the recorded version of the scene.

Yours sincerely,

Jennie Tyson

Jennie Tyson.

	TUESDAY	WEDNESDAY
9.15	4'A Rm T	4'A Rm O
9.55	4'A Rm T	1 2B Rm U
10.35	1 2B Rm U	1 2B Rm U
BREAK		
11.35	3'C Rm N	U6 Rm C
12.15	2 3A Rm T	U6 Rm C
12.55		
LUNCH		
2.10	FREE	3'C Rm T
2.30	5'D Rm T	3'C Rm T

Pupils required for filming : Tuesday 5th May 1.30pm-5.30pm

P. Butcher   )
F. Leigh   )
G. Wood   )
K. Lewis   )   T. Payne
S. Marshall   ) 5/1D   F. Mills   )
H. MacDonald   )   R. Price   )
J. James   )   D. Ransome   ) 5/2A
L. Bailey   )   J. Weaver   )

89

Mr McBrain

'I am utterly opposed to this whole idea. The film will give the school a very bad name. Lessons will be disrupted and the pupils taking part will miss a lot of important work.'

Ms Pearce

'I think its a wonderful idea. It will give the pupils a chance to have first-hand experience of the media, and it will give the public an insight into an ordinary school.'

Tuesday 5th May

The IBC TV crew turned up today – lorries and vans everywhere! Mr McBrain was very angry because when he arrived at school (late as usual!) there was a TV van stuck right across his parking place. That was only the start ...

Wednesday 6th May

SCHOOL STARS IN TV DRAMA

The pupils and buildings of St Peter's High School are this week making local history. St Peter's is the scene for an exciting new TV drama series being made by IBC TV . . .

Assignments

1 Study the material on pages 86 and 87. Mr Hadland has to 'sell this idea to the teachers.' He decides to write a letter to each teacher explaining what is planned and why he has agreed to it. Write the letter.

2 Study the material on pages 88 and 89. Work out the ways in which Mr McBrain's work will be affected on Tuesday and Wednesday. He decides to go to the Headmaster to complain. What does he say?

3 (Page 90) Mr McBrain and Ms Pearce have an argument in the staffroom about the TV project. Write the script of what they say.

4 The diary on page 90 is by a member of the 5th form who has been chosen to act in the play as an extra. Write his/her diary for Tuesday and Wednesday.

5 Write the full story printed in the newspaper under the heading 'School Stars in TV Drama'.

Compulsory Schooling?

The Law

1944 Education Act

Section 36:
It shall be the duty of the parent of every child of compulsory school age to cause him to receive efficient full-time education suitable to his age, ability and aptitude, and to any special educational needs he may have, either by regular attendance at school or otherwise.

Section 76:
In the exercise and performance of all powers and duties conferred and imposed on them by this Act the Minister and local education authorities shall have regard to the general principle that, so far as is compatible with the provision of efficient instruction and training and the avoidance of unreasonable public expenditure, pupils are to be educated in accordance with the wishes of their parents.

United Nations Universal Declaration of Human Rights

1 Everyone has a right to education.

2 Education shall be directed to the full development of the human personality.

3 Parents shall have prior right to choose the kind of education that shall be given to their children.

European Convention for the Protection of Human Rights and Fundamental Freedoms

No person shall be denied the right to education. In the exercise of any function which it assumes in relation to education and to teaching, the state shall respect the right of parents to ensure such education and teaching is in conformity with their own religious and philosophical convictions.

Taken from *School Is Not Compulsory* published by Education Otherwise

It's soon after daybreak. There's flour to be ground, bread to be baked and the chickens to be fed – the start of a typical day in the life of the Harrison family. They live in a tiny smallholding nestling in the shadow of the hills near Tenbury Wells, Worcestershire. But it is this daily routine, or rather lack of routine, that threatens the happiness of this family of six with its two dogs, six cats and a cow.

The children are being educated at home, but Geoff and Iris Harrison have been given an ultimatum by the local education authority: 'Show evidence that the children are being suitably educated for their age, aptitude and ability or send them to school.' Deadline is next Monday.

It is a battle the family has fought with the authorities since the eldest child, Wanda, 16, came of school age. In a sense the family has won. For now Wanda is beyond school age; the second daughter, Andrea, is 15; Grant is 13, and the youngest, Newall, is 9. A brighter and more able family of children is hard to imagine. Mr Harrison, a heating engineer, and his wife, a grammar school girl who became a fashion model, are convinced that their children are being brought up, however informally, in a manner that will equip them for life in the twentieth century far better than most children being put through the State system.

The children themselves, articulate, bright and with the sort of respect for their parents and each other rarely found these days, say they will never go to school. Although they have many friends they tend to find children of their own age 'silly about pop and things like that'.

While the family pretends to be unperturbed by the local authority's threat, there is no doubt that a cloud is hanging over them. In the past the authorities have threatened to take the children into care. 'When I think of the life my children lead and then read of others battered and maltreated I go cold with fright,' says Mrs Harrison, whose life is devoted to her family and its problems.

Two years ago, she thought she had won the legal battle over the children's education. But it seems she was wrong. A spokesman for Hereford and Worcester Education County Council said an attendance order had been served on the family following a meeting of the education committee which heard reports from education officers and social workers. 'We want evidence that the children are being educated suitably for their ages, aptitude and ability. If that cannot be given the children must be sent to school or legal action will follow.'

To this Mrs Harrison says: 'Then a court will have to decide what education is.'

When I called on the Harrisons, Wanda, Grant and Newall were hard at work shovelling earth to divide a fish tank they are building in which they hope to have some 3,000 rainbow trout. Andrea, who had just returned from a violin lesson, was studying shorthand. She has already taught herself to touch-type as has her sister.

Scattered about the old farmhouse were dozens of examples of the family's creative work – wool spun from the fleece of local sheep, woven rugs, intricately worked tapestries and garments that would enhance any Chelsea boutique.

Wanda prefers the outdoor life. She has tried her hand at wood-turning and loves growing things. The day I was there she had potted several dozen plants for selling at the local market and put some exotic seeds – birds of paradise and yellow guava – in her propagator.

The boys' first task of the day was to clean out and feed the chickens. Given a few chicks, Grant bred and reared 60 hens. He also built their runs. Now the birds have provided him with a successful business which produces some 40 eggs a day. 'It was the best way to teach him maths,' says his mother. He keeps his own books and is showing his younger brother how to do the same. 'They learn what is required. And they learn when they want to.'

Mrs Harrison knows that if she left home tomorrow the house would run smoothly with no squabbles over who does what and no nonsense about not knowing how to do it.

The whole, evidently successful, method of education goes back to Wanda's first traumatic days at school when she had difficulty with reading. The authorities wanted to send her to a school for the educationally sub-normal. But her mother taught her to read through the phonetic methods of shorthand.

As their father did as a child, the Harrison family have experienced reading problems, one of the reasons why their parents were not anxious to put them through the state system. 'There is no question of their being educationally sub-normal, but they have problems which I believe I can cope better with in the home than in any school situation,' says Mrs Harrison. At 9, Newall does not enjoy reading, 'but he will learn when he wants to and needs to'. Grant, too, has reading problems, but he is mastering them with the support of his sisters and his mother's enthusiasm.

When I asked the children if they would be photographed in the trap they have made for their pony they refused. Grant said: 'We are not something strange. We don't want to be pointed at in the market place. We just want to get on with our lives.'

I left thinking they were living just the kind of creative life thousands of city dwellers crave as they cram into their tube trains – a life where children are never bored and where coping with everyday problems rather than illusory ones is of prime importance.

If the case reaches the courts the magistrates will be faced with the unenviable task of deciding what is right for the Harrison children.

Brenda Parry, *Daily Telegraph* 30 April 1979

Cross-Examination _____

In his play *Flying into the Wind*, David Leland tells the story of a family very similar to the Harrisons. The Wyatts are prosecuted for not sending their son Michael to school, even though their daughter, who is older, has been educated at home very successfully. In this scene, Michael's mother, Sally, is being cross-examined by the prosecution lawyer.

HEALEY   How is your approach different to the approach of a school?

SALLY WYATT   First, we concentrate on what they can do, rather than what they cannot do. We follow the needs of the child.

HEALEY   I'm not at all sure what you mean by that, Mrs Wyatt: how exactly does one do that – 'follow the needs of the child?'

SALLY WYATT   I've already explained. Our society isn't in the habit of following the needs of the child, that's why we give them things like concrete playgrounds; they fit the needs of the adult.

HEALEY   Yes, but I still have no clear picture of how your approach of 'following the child' differs from that of the average school.

SALLY WYATT   Well, we don't have a curriculum for a start, we don't have a set routine, we don't sit down and do lessons. Whereas a school would concentrate on what the child finds difficult, we concentrate on what they enjoy doing; we don't set standards, we don't give them so many marks out of ten.

HEALEY   Who decides on what activity is to be followed?

SALLY WYATT   They do. They must decide for themselves.

HEALEY   They are allowed to follow whatever activity they choose.

SALLY WYATT   Yes.

HEALEY   For as long as they like?

SALLY WYATT   Yes.

HEALEY   And no one ever corrects them, even if they've made the wrong decision.

SALLY WYATT   The best way to discover that is through experience, not by being told not to do something. The essence of learning is experience. Children are very quick to abandon what does not interest them.

HEALEY   Don't you feel that sometimes they must be made to face a difficult task in order to learn?

SALLY WYATT	No, never. They must set their own standards.
HEALEY	So, in your system – if it is a system – children do not have to measure up to any objective standards in what they are doing. If they set out to do a task, they are free to abandon it if they wish to, or to continue it as long as they like and nobody will stop, correct or guide them in any way – is that correct?
SALLY WYATT	We don't tell our children what to do or how to do it; they must take their own decisions.
HEALEY	Let us take an example. Suppose Michael wanted to go fishing all day – some children will go fishing all day and every day, if given the chance – what would you do?
SALLY WYATT	We don't make the kind of distinctions between work and play which are behind the question.
HEALEY	That is a very idealistic and somewhat patronizing answer to a very simple question. If Michael wanted to go out fishing every day, what would you do?
SALLY WYATT	It just doesn't happen, not like that. It's difficult ... you see, I think it's difficult for us to understand this. We have been brought up with the feeling that work takes one away from the things one really enjoys. Why should it be like this? It's not like that for them.
JUDGE WOOD	Mrs Wyatt, what you are really being asked is, as I understand it, is there anyone who can tell Michael if he is right or not? Do you follow?
SALLY WYATT	They are self-assessing, Your Honour. They decide how well they are doing. It is success or failure on their own terms, nobody else's. We say to our children, 'only you have the answers to your own lives'. That has nothing to do with dyslexia. It's not a soft approach, it's very tough. The world is changing quickly and violently – they must have the ability to control their own lives and create their own standards. It takes time and effort to create an environment where children can find out, where they can discover themselves. Just as it has taken time and effort to deprive them of that privilege and to construct an educational system where they are given the idea that parents, teachers, somebody, anybody other than themselves, has got all the answers and that their part in that is simply to do as they're told, to sit back and wait for the information to be vended to them.
HEALEY	And yet Michael is eleven and cannot read.
SALLY WYATT	Not yet.

David Leland, *Flying into the Wind*

SPLIT RULING ON TUITION OF CHILDREN

A judge yesterday ruled that a family educating their children on their smallholding had provided satisfactory tuition for their daughter, but not for their two sons.

Judge Ward allowed an appeal by Mr and Mrs Geoffrey Harrison of Rochford, Tenbury, Worcestershire, against a conviction for failing to send their daughter, Andrea, now aged 17, to school. But he refused to allow similar appeals in respect of their two sons, Grant, now aged 15 and Newall, aged 11.

Mr and Mrs Harrison have been fighting in the courts for eight years for their right to educate their children in their own way without interference from the local authority. They say the children suffer from dyslexia and have difficulty in reading and writing.

Judge Ward, announcing a reserved judgment at Hereford Crown Court, said he was satisfied that the system of project learning adopted by Mr and Mrs Harrison had been adequate in many respects. He said: 'This is a case of responsible and caring parents doing what they believe to be best for their children.'

But he criticised Mrs Harrison for refusing to have her children monitored by officials from Hereford and Worcester Education Authority.

But Judge Ward pointed out that Andrea Harrison could read and write, write shorthand and read music, and in his view she was 'educated' within the terms of the law.

He had reservations in the cases of the boys because of their inability to read and write competently. Because he felt that that was an essential factor in an education, he rejected the appeals.

The Times 2 June 1981

Assignments

The law

1 Copy the following table. If the item has something to say about the particular subject, put a tick. If not, put a cross.

	Rights of parents	Duties of parents	Rights of children	Where children should be educated	Duties of government
1944 Act					
UN Declaration					
European Convention					

2 For each of the following statements say whether it is true or false and why.
- (a) Children in Britain *must* go to school.
- (b) According to the UN Declaration parents have the right to choose where their children shall be educated.
- (c) In Britain parents have complete freedom to decide how their children shall be educated.

Education Otherwise

Read the report carefully and then explain briefly what it says about each of these points:
- (a) what the Harrisons believe about education;
- (b) their lifestyle;
- (c) how they have been treated by the local education authority;
- (d) the reporter's general attitude towards them.

Cross-examination

In the extract, Mrs Wyatt is questioned by someone who is hostile to her beliefs. During the trial she is also questioned by her own lawyer, whose aim is to give her an opportunity to explain fully and clearly what she believes in and what she thinks is wrong with the education offered by schools. Write the script of that part of the trial.

The whole unit

Think about your own attitude to the issues raised in this unit. Then write an expression of your views.

Weather Forecasts

How Accurate Are Weather Forecasts? _____

British weather is notoriously variable. We've looked at where to find the best weather forecasts and how to get the most out of the weather maps.

The Meteorological Office claims to get them right about 85% of the time, which is pretty good when you consider how variable our weather can be.

We found that the forecasts we monitored were acceptable for most practical purposes 88% of the time. But errors and local variations meant that they were accurate for *all* practical purposes much less often – about half the time.

What goes wrong?

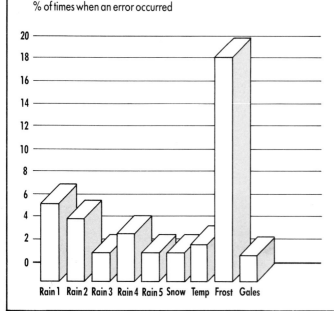

% of times when an error occurred

Key

Rain 1 – Timing error of 6 hours or more
Rain 2 – Amount seriously underestimated
Rain 3 – Amount seriously overestimated
Rain 4 – Widespread **showers**/thunderstorms underestimated
Rain 5 – Widespread showers/thunderstorms overestimated
Snow – Seriously underestimated
Temp – Major error of temperature
Frost – Not forecast
Gales – Severe gales underestimated

Text and information from **Which?** August 1985

How Helpful Are Different Forecasts? _____

Slowly but surely as the strong winds and thicker cloud take hold of the country, temperatures are returning to more usual values for early October. Some rain to come for all of you today, so for the details I'll look at South East and Central England, the Midlands, East Anglia and Lincolnshire, also the Channel Islands. It's rather cloudy with some light rain in some places. The rain'll die away; it'll be fairly bright this morning with just a little sunshine in the eastern counties. It'll cloud over again by the afternoon with some more definite rain coming along and there'll be some pockets of heavier rain, too. Temperatures 17 to 19 degrees Celsius.

For South West England, Wales, and all northern counties of England it's cloudy; there's some rain around already and some of that rain'll get quite persistent and heavy. It'll turn brighter and showery from the West later, though with the showers running quickly along on the blustery wind, so there'll be some sunshine in between the showers. Temperatures this afternoon 17 or 18 Celsius.

In Northern Ireland and the Isle of Man it's cloudy; there's rain around – some of the rain's quite heavy. It'll turn brighter and showery through the morning with some sunshine, but when the showers come along they're going to be quite heavy and thundery and quite squally. Temperatures 16 Celsius at best and the temperatures may even fall later this afternoon.

Finally for Scotland: it's wet in Shetland now, but you'll have a dry period later. However there's more rain getting into south-western regions now and it'll sweep quickly across all of Scotland followed by brighter conditions and blustery showers and just a little sunshine in a few places. The showers will turn out to be heavy, possibly prolonged and thundery, and quite squally too. Temperatures 15 or 16 Celsius. And the winds over the country south or south-westerly; they're quite a feature – quite fresh or strong everywhere and with gale force winds over the hills and around some coasts.

Tonight there'll be clear periods, continuing strong winds and a few blustery showers more especially in Western and Northern areas. On Friday some showers, some of them heavy, but also some sunshine, but more general rain coming along for Saturday.

And that's the weather forecast.

BBC Radio 4 Weather Forecast, 06.55 hours, 3 October 1985

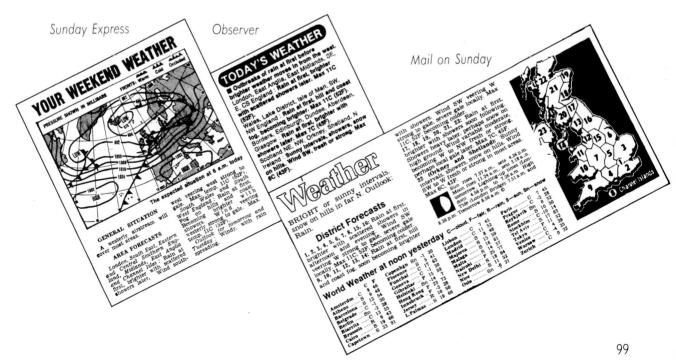

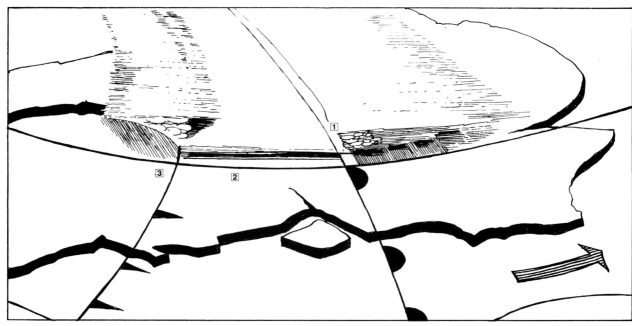

1 WARM FRONT APPROACHES
Cloud increases, temperature rises and there's a long period of rain so the warm front slowly approaches. Pressure drops and wind speed increases as the isobars get closer together.

2 BETWEEN THE FRONTS
Warm air, rain ceases, may be clear, but often drizzly. The wind direction changes from SE to SW.

3 COLD FRONT PASSES
Unsettled air, tall thick clouds, squally rain, possible thunder. The pressure rises again as the front passes over, leaving cooler but closer weather.

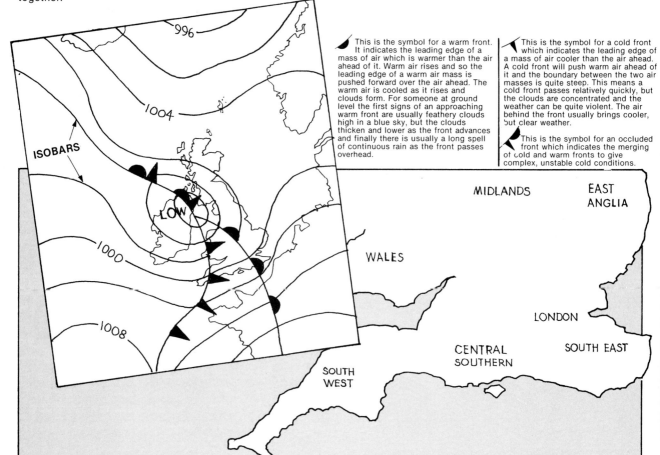

This is the symbol for a warm front. It indicates the leading edge of a mass of air which is warmer than the air ahead of it. Warm air rises and so the leading edge of a warm air mass is pushed forward over the air ahead. The warm air is cooled as it rises and clouds form. For someone at ground level the first signs of an approaching warm front are usually feathery clouds high in a blue sky, but the clouds thicken and lower as the front advances and finally there is usually a long spell of continuous rain as the front passes overhead.

This is the symbol for a cold front which indicates the leading edge of a mass of air cooler than the air ahead. A cold front will push warm air ahead of it and the boundary between the two air masses is quite steep. This means a cold front passes relatively quickly, but the clouds are concentrated and the weather can be quite violent. The air behind the front usually brings cooler, but clear weather.

This is the symbol for an occluded front which indicates the merging of cold and warm fronts to give complex, unstable cold conditions.

Assignments

Preparatory work

Study the material in each section and then answer these questions.

How accurate are weather forecasts?

1 What are the forecasts best at forecasting?
2 What are the forecasts worst at forecasting?
3 In each of these the forecasts were quite often wrong:
Rain 1; Rain 2; Rain 4; Frost.
Who would be most seriously affected by errors in these forecasts?

How helpful are different forecasts?

1 Which forecast provides the most information?
2 Which forecast provides the least information?
3 Which forecast is easiest to understand quickly?
4 Which forecast is hardest to understand quickly?

Interpreting a weather map
What will the weather be in each of these regions?

London and the South East.
Central Southern.
South West.

Writing

How accurate are weather forecasts?

Write an argument between two people. One thinks that weather forecasts are really pretty good. The other thinks that they ought to be a lot better. Use the information in this section. Write the argument as a script.

How helpful are different weather forecasts?

Use the *information* in the radio forecast to write forecasts in the *style* of
(a)   The *Observer,*
(b)   The *Mail on Sunday,*
(c)   The *Sunday Express.*

Interpreting a weather map

Use the information provided by the maps to write weather forecasts:
(a)   for BBC Radio 4;
(b)   for one of the newspapers quoted on page 99

Scenes of Conflict

The material in this unit comes from a leaflet produced by Oxfam. The main work is at the end of the unit, but at the bottom of each page there are notes and questions to guide your reading.

1 What is the purpose of this page?
2 Which countries are mentioned?
3 What have they in common?

Removals — so-called "black spots" are isolated enclaves of settled black communities with freehold land, which they have occupied since the turn of the century, but which is surrounded by white owned land. Under the apartheid system they are threatened with removal to "homeland" or "bantustan" areas.

Hopewell is a "black spot" in Natal. The community of 4,000 is under threat of removal although they have been settled there since 1901. Oxfam has contributed £3,571 to build a water system to pump water to the village. By sponsoring community organised programmes such as this one, Oxfam helps to consolidate and strengthen the community in its resolve to resist removal.

The repression and violence of apartheid directly hits at the work you support. In 1981 an Oxfam co-worker and his wife were detained and tortured. The current partial state of emergency has witnessed an upsurge in detentions and deaths and Oxfam has supported humanitarian relief work arising from the unrest in black townships.

For example we have made a £15,000 grant to the South African Council of Churches' emergency fund to help the families of those killed, hurt or detained.

When Muslim Amal militiamen took over the Sabra and Shatilla camps — the homes of thousands of Palestinian refugees — a further refugee crisis was created in **LEBANON**. The disruption and trauma of the fighting and its aftermath were extreme. Oxfam has made a number of small grants since the fighting in May totalling around £5,000.

These include a grant for rubble clearance in Shatilla, grants to give emergency relief to people who fled Sabra and Shatilla, including one of those who fled to the city of Sidon in Southern Lebanon, and a grant to assist in the cleaning of the increasingly unhygienic, overcrowded garages, basements and unfinished buildings which were occupied during the very hottest part of the summer by Palestinian refugees.

1 What is Oxfam's attitude to apartheid?
2 What is the purpose of advice offices?
3 What is SADWA?

The scourges of war, repression and inter-communal violence threaten poor people in many of the countries in which Oxfam works. Here we focus on projects working in the shadow of violent conflict.

In 1984–85 Oxfam committed over £300,000 to projects in **SOUTH AFRICA**. Our policy in South Africa is based on our perception that apartheid is the major obstacle to development for the poor. Here are some of the areas in which we work:

Advice offices — located in black townships or down-city areas, these help people with pension, disability or workers' compensation claims and with unemployment claims and the problems created by the myriad of apartheid laws and passbook regulations which control black peoples' lives.

Domestic workers — there are an estimated 1 million domestics or "maids" in South Africa and they represent one of the most disadvantaged groups of workers. Oxfam supports the South Africa Domestic Workers Association. Run by former domestic workers, SADWA aims to protect domestics against exploitation and secure fair and reasonable conditions of employment.

1   What is a 'black spot', and what can Oxfam do to help?
2   How is Oxfam's work affected by apartheid?
3   Sabra and Shatilla are camps for refugees in Lebanon. How have they been affected by the recent conflict?
4   How has Oxfam helped?

REPORTING FROM SCENES OF CONFLICT

Since the renewed strife between Tamil and Sinhalese communities that broke out in July 1983 Oxfam has been involved in **SRI LANKA** with a substantial programme of relief and rehabilitation.

A

B

C

D

E

On this page most of the text has been removed. The five large letters show where the main sections were. On the next page there is an exercise based on this.

Assignments

Note-making and summarising

1 Make notes on the ways in which Oxfam has helped in South Africa.

2 Use your notes to write a paragraph of about 100 words explaining what Oxfam has done in South Africa.

Writing the text

You have been asked to write the text for the page about Sri Lanka (page 105). You have to write so that your text fits the space available.

Section A: 100 words
Section B: 30 words
Section C: 40 words
Section D: 40 words
Section E: 60 words

Use these notes to write your text:

A
1 Militant Tamils fighting government
Security forces hit back at Tamil civilians
"Climate of Terror" – Marcus Thompson (Oxfam)
2 Most people helped by Oxfam are Tamils
But some are Sinhalese too.
3 Relief supplies provided through local groups
Helping people get back to work too

B
Trincomalee Area

People's homes destroyed in disturbances
£14,000 to build houses (wattle and daub)

C
Trincomalee

People fled in disturbances
Lost everything
Returned – nothing
£5,500 given for seed so they can plant

D
Batticaloa District

£8,000 - cooking utensils for 25,000 refugees
£8,000 - to buy land, build houses, toilets, well,
children's centre

E

1 Jaffna Peninsula

Tamils fled from south
£14,000 for clothing for 2000 families

2 General Comment

Situation very serious
Oxfam opening local office – quicker and more effective response

Making a poster

The material in this leaflet is very detailed. Decide what its most important message is. Design a poster to get that message across in secondary schools. The poster below will give you some ideas.

Flour power.

Give the poor the power to grow their own food.

Christian Aid ⊕ P.O. Box 1, London SW9. THE CHURCHES IN ACTION WITH THE WORLD'S POOR

Harztours

How It Started ...

TRAVEL COURIER

HARZIAN
CONSULATE

The Government of Harzia wishes to create a new government tourist office, HarzTours, in London to promote British tourism in Harzia. Applications are invited from suitable qualified persons for the post of Manager. Applicants should have some experience of the travel business and should be young and enthusiastic. Particularly in the early stages, the job will involve travelling between Britain and Harzia and conducting parties of tourists round Harzia. Applicants are invited to write a preliminary letter setting out details of relevant experience and interests and explaining briefly why they are interested in the post.

Address for correspondence: The Information Officer, Harzian Consulate, 1 Piccadilly, London.

HARZIAN
CONSULATE

1 Piccadilly
London

Ref: 19okf/45/84

15 November 1984

Dear Sir,

Following your recent interview with us in connection with your application for the post of Manager, HarzTours, I am pleased to inform you that you have been selected for the post. I shall be grateful if you will write confirming that you wish to...

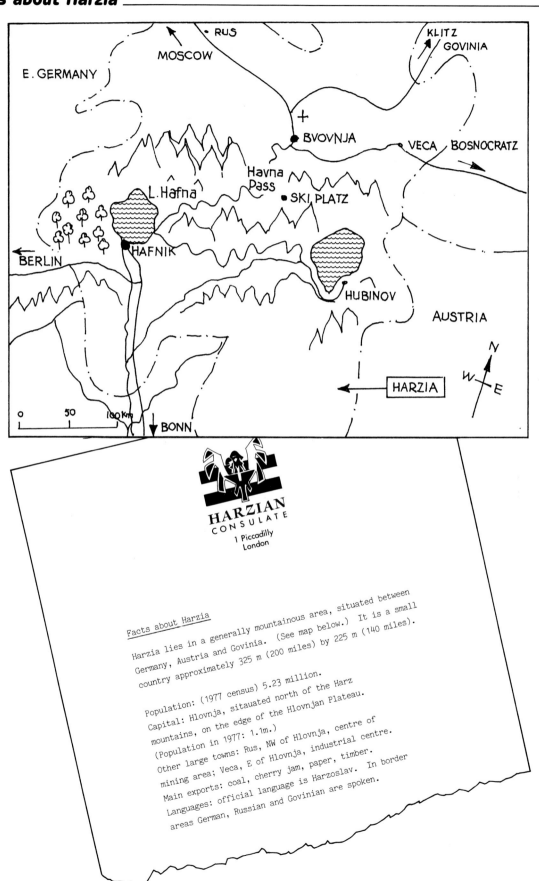

HARZIAN
CONSULATE
1 Piccadilly
London

Facts about Harzia

Harzia lies in a generally mountainous area, situated between Germany, Austria and Govinia. (See map below.) It is a small country approximately 325 m (200 miles) by 225 m (140 miles).

Population: (1977 census) 5.23 million.
Capital: Hlovnja, situated north of the Harz mountains, on the edge of the Hlovnjan Plateau. (Population in 1977: 1.1m.)
Other large towns: Rus, NW of Hlovnja, centre of mining area; Veca, E of Hlovnja, industrial centre.
Main exports: coal, cherry jam, paper, timber.
Languages: official language is Harzoslav. In border areas German, Russian and Govinian are spoken.

Views of Harzia

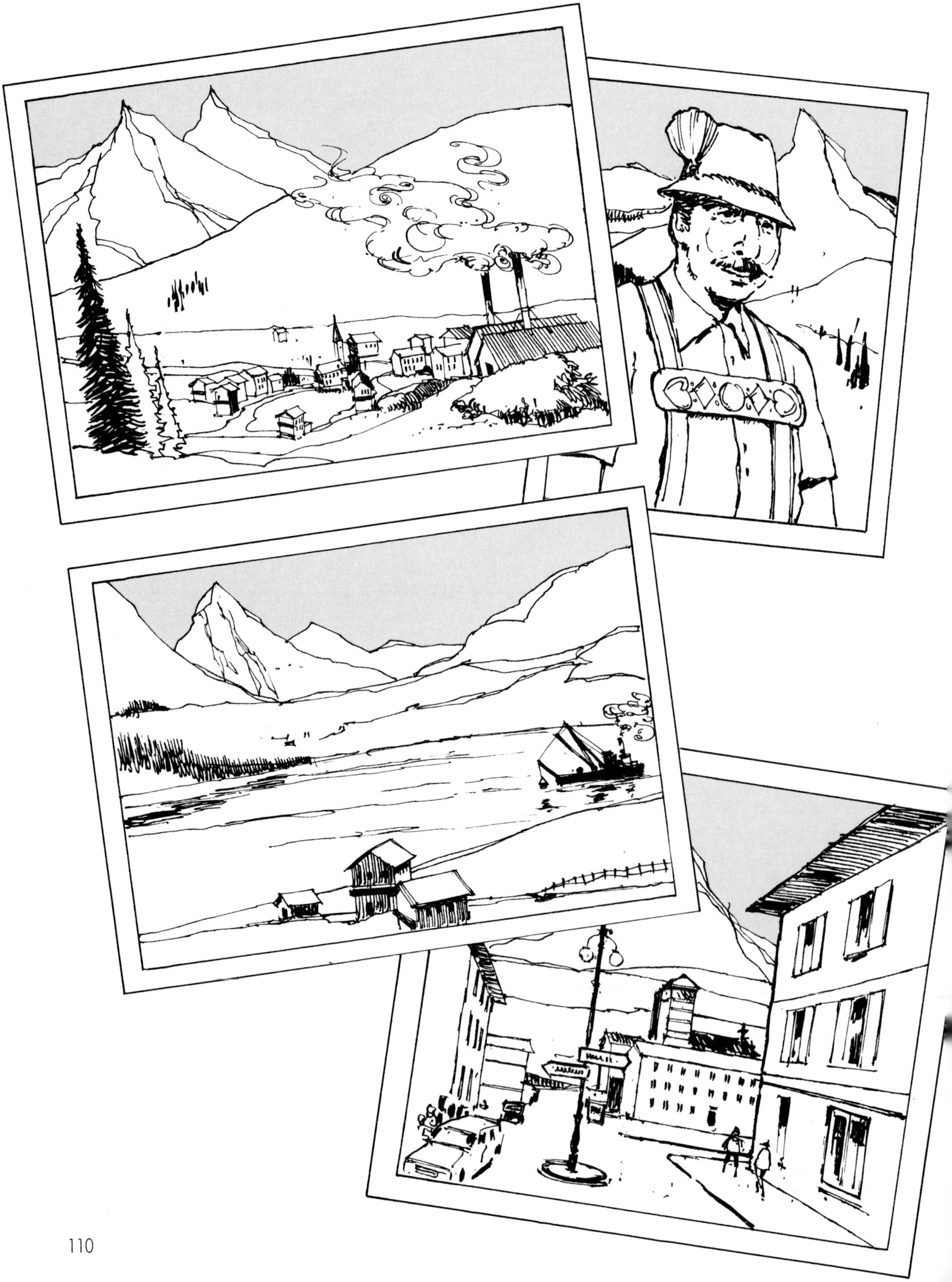

The climate of Hafnik

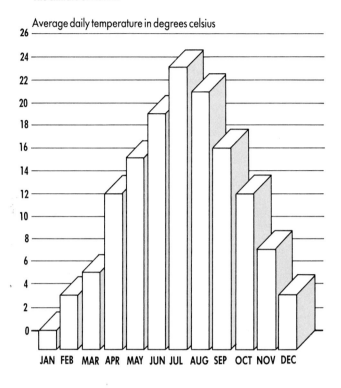

Average daily temperature in degrees celsius

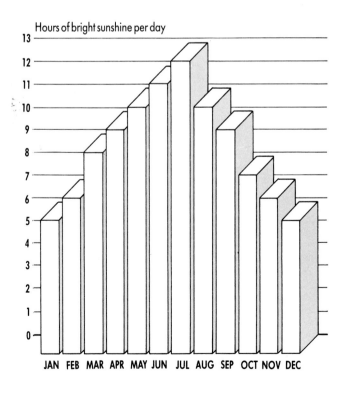

Hours of bright sunshine per day

HARZIAN
CONSULATE
1 Piccadilly
London

WELCOMES TO HARZIA!!

Welcomes to Harzia the new Europeanish tourism zentrum! Harzia is a homeland of mountains and trees, water and snow. The people are warm and offer you a friendly. So come and greet us now!

Harzia is a small country but with much varieties of the paysage. To the north is the urban of Hlovnja on the Hlovnja Platorsk with important industriels zentrum. The touristic is all to the southern mountains area. Here is abundance of hill, tree, water and - importantest - tranquil Nature.

Two great lake, Hafna and hubi, give you watersport angle swim and view. The eastern, Hafna, is in flat area with heavy wooded and much bird. The western Hubi is rung by mountain with wounder vista and many long-distance-walk for the energyman.

In wintertime the mountain show like a white blanket. From novembre through april is oppirtunity for the ski, wintersport and not forgetting the glamorous after-ski. New wintersport zentrum are being made above Hubinov and at Skiplatz in mid mountain area.

Cold or hot, up or down, Harzia is for thee!

Assignments

1 Write a letter of application for the post of Manager, Harztours, London.
2 Write a revised version of the draft advertisement 'Welcomes to Harzia' in good English.
3 Use the material in this unit to make up a short brochure advertising summer holidays in Southern Harzia. You should include the following:
   (a) general information about the area;
   (b) particular holiday opportunities;
   (c) the weather;
   (d) which pictures you would use from those on page 110 ;
   (e) captions for the pictures;
   (f) details of specific package tours offered.

Postscript

TERRORISTS THREATEN TOURIST PLAN

WEDNESDAY, JUNE

Harzian government facing serious problems. The plan of the new Harzian government to open the country up to tourists suffered another setback yesterday. The terrorist group FLASH (Front for the Liberation of Southern Harzia) attacked a vital roadbridge near Hafnik and threatened to blow up a large section of the main road to Bonn and Berlin unless their demands are met. FLASH, who represent politicians and others ousted in the recent change of government in Harzia, are asking for the creation of a separate state of Hafna, independent of the rest of Harzia. Hafnik is the main town in the area which the government wish to promote as a tourist area. It is situated on the vital route from East and West Germany to the rest of Harzia. If FLASH cause major disruption then the Harzia Government will be unable to proceed with the development of a major new tourist industry . . .

Assignment

Imagine that you are on one of the first package tours to Harzia. Your tour gets caught up in the activities of the terrorists. Write the story of what happens.

Cities in Crisis

The cities of the developing world are growing so fast that they are bursting at the seams. Seventy-five thousand people *per day* move from the countryside into the cities. Most of them go to live in shanty towns. These are areas of do-it-yourself housing, built mostly from corrugated iron, packing cases and plastic sheeting. They encircle most cities in the developing world. In some cases up to two-thirds or even three-quarters of the whole population of a city may be housed in such areas.

The environment in which such city-dwellers live is dirty and dangerous. In 1980, 177,000,000 did not have clean water to drink and nearly twice that number had no proper sanitation. There is a shortage of food and fuel, and illness and accidents are common.

Although life in the cities of the north is nothing like so wretched, these, too, face serious problems. While cities in the developing world are pushing outwards, those of the north are decaying in the centre. Industry is declining and many rich people have already moved out into the comfortable (and expensive) outer suburbs They leave behind the poor, the old and ethnic minorities in the city centres. This means that there is less income for the city councils, who have to reduce the services they provide. This leads even more people to leave the centre and so the problem gets worse.

Contrasts in a Third World city: the wealthy central area viewed from the poverty of an outer shanty town.

The worm inside the rotten Apple

My reluctant thesis is that New York is the city of Attila the Hun, a city tolerant of devastation and death. Anyone who has lived in New York has his own memory of horror stories. Five people stabbed one morning at my nearest subway station. Two boys, to get their revenge on a subway clerk who had stopped them jumping turnstiles, returned with petrol and burned the woman to death: this is a practice known as torching. A 14-year-old boy shot to death for his bicycle, and his sister asking, 'Couldn't they just have shot him in the leg?' This last case gets the essence of the whole criminal city - that violence is expected and accepted. "But couldn't they just have shot him in the leg ?''

There is one's own experience. I have lived in four apartments in New York, and although all were by London standards heavily armoured, one needing three keys and a knowledge of the burglar alarm to enter, both that one and another were burgled.

And so it could go on. The afternoon of one burglary of mine, two people were taken away dead on the same block, one from an overdose of drugs, one from knife wounds. The last two days of my last visit, a 14-year-old was accused of the murder of a 17-year-old because the older boy had stabbed him the month before. In a Brooklyn subway station a man, having been taunted by younger men, threw a cop onto the tracks and tried to shoot two others. The cops shot him, and as he lay on the platform, a young man, practising what he described as his Kung Fu technique, kicked him and jumped on his back, and the man died on his way to hospital.

Terry Coleman, *Guardian* 9 August 1985

Housing action, North
1 Newly built community centre and day nursery run by local people.
2 Modern infill housing for sale, supported by low-cost home ownership scheme.
3, 4, 5 Renovation – through improvement grants for private owners, or undertaken by non-profit agency, or city government.
6 New extensions for bathrooms and kitchens.
7 Street uplift – speed humps, controlled parking, landscapes

8 Community art – murals decorating blank walls, painted by community artist and local children.
9 Corner shops retained for local shopping – also for use as Neighbourhood Office of city government.
10 New neighbourhood park with children's playground.
11 Unimproved terrace awaiting action.
12 Small workshop development for locally based employment.
13 Local bus transport.

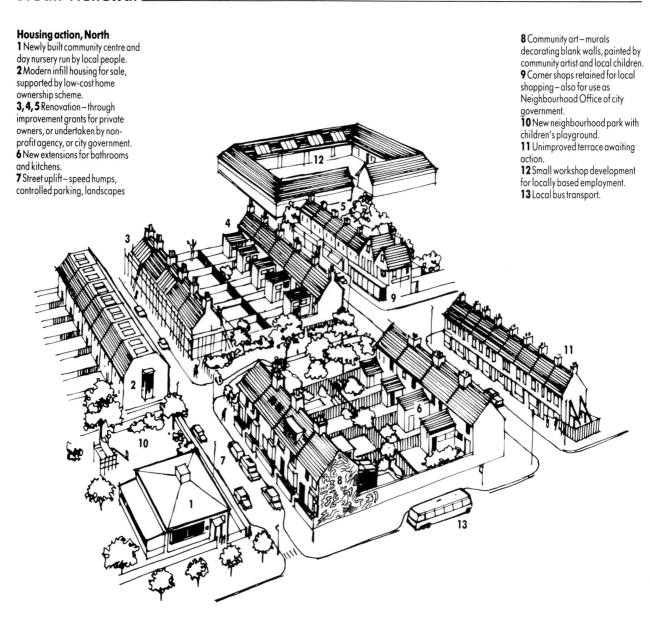

Rehabilitating northern cities

1 Build a 'village in the city'.
2 Base renewal on communities that already exist.
3 Local people can do a lot, but Government help essential.
4 Existing houses have to be renovated.
5 New buildings to be designed to match what's already there.
6 Old factories to be converted to new use (light industry, craft workshops, etc.).
7 New community centres, small shops.
8 Car-free areas, tree planting and gardens.

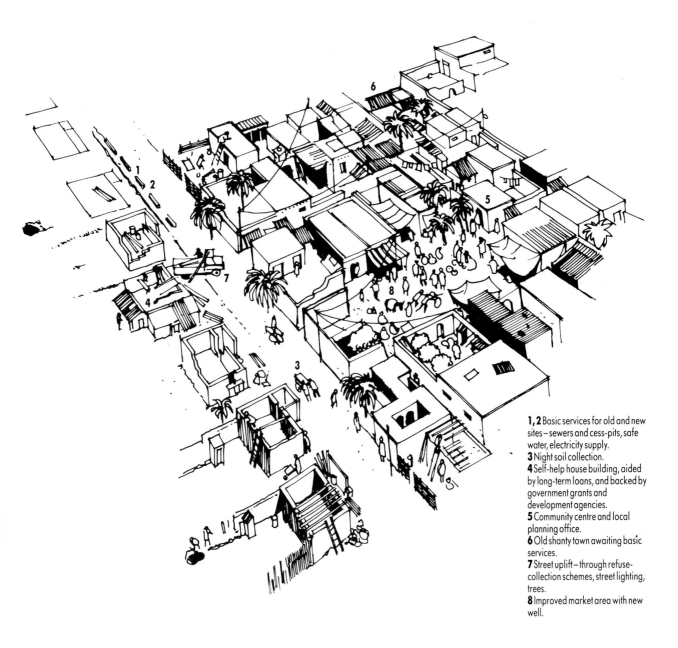

1,2 Basic services for old and new sites – sewers and cess-pits, safe water, electricity supply.
3 Night soil collection.
4 Self-help house building, aided by long-term loans, and backed by government grants and development agencies.
5 Community centre and local planning office.
6 Old shanty town awaiting basic services.
7 Street uplift – through refuse-collection schemes, street lighting, trees.
8 Improved market area with new well.

Rescuing southern cities

1 Main problem: providing essential services.
2 Water, sanitation, electric power.
3 Leave house construction to settlers.
4 Improve some other things, e.g. markets.
5 No solution if people continue to flood in.
6 Essential to improve conditions in countryside.

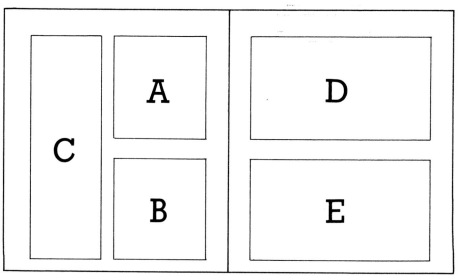

Pages 114 and 115

Assignments

Preparatory work
Finding your way around

1   Look at the double page *as a whole*. It contains these items:

        cartoon
        information about cities in the developed world ('the North')
        information about cities in the developing world ('the South')
        stories about crime and violence in New York
        photograph of city in the North
        photograph of city in the South

    Which is which?

2   Study the items carefully *one at a time*.

3   In which item(s) can you find information about the following?
    (a)   the growth of cities in the developing world
    (b)   shanty towns
    (c)   the decay of cities in the developing world
    (d)   crime in the cities of the North
    (e)   why people in the South move from the countryside to the cities

Questions on items A, B and C

1   What is a shanty town?

2   Why do so many people in the South move from the countryside into cities?

3   Explain in your own words the medical problems faced by people in shanty towns and the causes for them.

4   Explain the social problems faced by people in Northern cities and the causes for them.

Writing

1   Give the cartoon a suitable title.

2   You are a member of a new charity which aims to help with the problems of cities in the developing world. Give the charity a name. Write a short (about 300 words) appeal statement explaining why you are collecting money and how it will be used.

3   On returning from New York Terry Coleman is interviewed on TV about his recent trip and his experiences. Use the information in the article to write an account of the conversation that takes place.

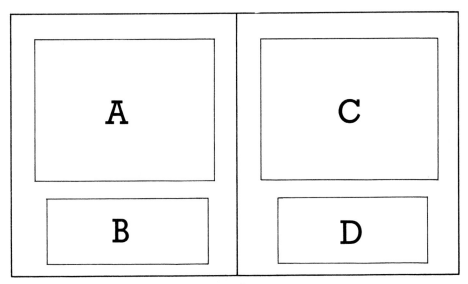

Pages 116 and 117

Preparatory work

These two pages contain detailed information about urban renewal. Study the diagrams carefully and make sure that you understand them before you tackle the writing assignments.

Writing

1 Item B is in note-form. Write a paragraph using the information and ideas it contains.
2 Use the information in item A to write a second paragraph continuing and developing the ideas in your first paragraph.
3 Do the same for items C and D

Writing about the unit as a whole

1 You have been asked to give a short talk about 'The Problems of the City and How People Are Trying To Solve Them'. Write the text of your talk.
2 Collect factual information on the themes of city problems and city renewal in an area near to where you live. Write a commentary on 'The City and its Problems' using the information you have collected.

Acknowledgements

The author and publishers wish to thank the following for permission to reproduce copyright material:

H.M.S.O. for statistics pp. 7, 9 and 10 from *Social Trends 1986*, and pp. 46, 82 and 83; Good Year Tyre & Rubber Company (Great Britain) Limited for advertisement p. 15 (supplied by McCann-Erickson Advertising Ltd); *New Internationalist* for article of 9/85; Jimmy Savile for article of 22/4/86 from Weekend Magazine; The Countryside Commission and H.M.S.O. Publications for details from *The Country Code*; *The Times* for the articles of 15/11/85 by Geoffrey Matthews, 2/6/81 and 18/4/86 by Stewart Tendler; *The Sun* for articles of 15/11/85 by Richard Ellis and 18/4/86 by Michael Felder; Datalink for advertisement p. 37; Virago Press Ltd for 'Recipe' by Carol Adams and Rae Laurikietis from The Gender Trap Book 1, Education and Work; Tunstall Lifeline and Boots the Chemist Ltd for advertisement p. 52; Stannah Lifts for advertisements p. 52 and p. 53 (supplied by Abucon International Business and Public Relations Consultants and Riggs Advertising Limited); Vessa Limited for advertisement p. 53; Everest & Jennings Ltd for advertisement p. 53; Fiat Auto UK Ltd for advertisement p. 61 (supplied by Davidson Pearce Limited © Nick Carding); Daihatsu (UK) Ltd for advertisement p. 58-9; Lada Cars for advertisement p. 60 (supplied by the Graham Poulter Partnership); Yugo Cars for the advertisement p. 62; Nissan UK for the advertisement p. 58; A. D. Peters & Co. Ltd for the cartoon 'We Bring You — Live, from the Scene of the Tragedy' by Posy Simmonds; Mirror Group Newspapers for article of 15/11/85 by Bob Graham and Christine Garbott; British Broadcasting Corporation for Radio 4 broadcast of 15/11/86 and weather forecast of 3/10/85; *Which?* magazine for report on Street Crime (11/85) and weather forecast (8/85); *The Observer* for article of 27/10/85 by Katherine Whitehorn and weather forecast of 19/1/86; Oxfam for articles pp. 102-105; RoSPA for details of the Cycling Proficiency Test; Education Otherwise for 'School is not compulsory'; *The Daily Telegraph* and Brenda Parry for article of 30/4/79; Cambridge University Press and David Leland for extract from the play 'Flying into the Wind'; *The Daily Express* for weather forecast of 19/1/86; *The Mail on Sunday* for weather forecast of 19/1/86; Allen & Unwin and Kevin Woodcock for illustrations from 'City Rules O.K.; Terry Coleman for extract from 'The Worm inside the Rotten Apple' from *The Guardian* 9/4/85; Pan Books Ltd for adaptations of illustrations from the *Gaia Atlas*.

It has not been possible in all cases to trace copyright-holders; the publishers would be glad to hear from any such unacknowledged copyright-holders.

We would also like to thank the following for supplying copyright photographs:
p. 12 Sporting Pictures; p. 13 (top) Popperfoto; p. 13 (bottom) and p. 91 Liz Somerville; p. 27 Coventry Evening Telegraph; p. 92 RoSPA.